CHILD-CENTERED PLAY THERAPY WORKBOOK

CHILD-CENTERED PLAY THERAPY WORKBOOK

A SELF-DIRECTED GUIDE FOR PROFESSIONALS

JODI ANN MULLEN
JUNE M. RICKLI

RESEARCH PRESS
PUBLISHERS

2612 North Mattis Avenue, Champaign, Illinois 61822
800.519.2707 / researchpress.com

RESEARCH PRESS
PUBLISHERS

PDF versions of forms and checklists included in this
book are available for download on the book webpage at
www.researchpress.com/downloads

Copies of this book may be ordered from Research Press at the address given on the title page.

Composition by Jeff Helgesen
Cover design by McKenzie Wagner, Inc.
Printed by Edwards Brothers Malloy

ISBN 978-0-87822-682-5
Library of Congress Catalog Number 2014900100

Contents

Acknowledgments

We would like to express our gratitude to all of the people who have both directly and indirectly helped us create this book. We are students of play therapy. We want to express our sincerest thanks to our teachers. Our teachers have come into our lives as our child clients and their parents, as well as our students and supervisees. Thank you for teaching us the most important and elusive lessons of play therapy.

We would also like to express our gratitude to our support systems at Integrative Counseling Services and in the Counseling and Psychological Services Department at SUNY Oswego. A special thank you to Kelly LaBarge, Jessica Connors, and Tiffany Tesoriero, who were all instrumental in helping us create this manual.

We are appreciative of Karen Steiner and Judy Parkinson at Research Press, who believed in our work and have provided us this incredible opportunity to share it.

Jodi writes . . .

I am so blessed to be doing the work I love with the people who matter most to me giving me their full support. Thank you, June, for agreeing to work on this project with me and bringing your expertise, creativity, sense of humor, and passion to the project. I am grateful for all that you share with me, most importantly your friendship.

I have the most awesome children! Thank you, Andrew and Leah, for being understanding and patient and for valuing my purpose. Not surprisingly, those awesome children have an awesome dad. I appreciate my husband, Michael. Thank you for believing in me and what's important to me. I am so lucky to have a partner who loves me the way you do.

June writes . . .

I would like to thank Jodi for the opportunity to be her coauthor for this book—the experience was a wonderful meshing of our personal and professional relationship. You have inspired, mentored, and shared your passion for play therapy with me, for which I'll always be grateful. My husband, Bill, has been a continuous and never wavering source of support in our 38 years together. You know how to motivate, inspire, and support me, and you also know when to lay low and let me figure it out on my own. I am extremely proud of our three children: Chris, Dan, and Kate. Thank you for putting up with our parenting bloopers and for becoming the awesome adults you are. Your experiences growing up have provided me with some great comic relief during teaching and supervision and in consultations with parents. Last, thank you to those throughout my life who doubted my ability—you have been my among my greatest motivators!

Introduction

What Is Play Therapy?

Play therapy provides a context for understanding children and their world views. In this workbook, the focus is on the child-centered play therapy philosophy and approach. Some elements of play therapy are, however, consistent across theoretical and/or applied play therapy approaches, and much from this workbook can be gleaned and applied to play therapy in general.

Play can be used in interventions to help practitioners understand the perspectives, behaviors, feelings, and thoughts of children (Ablon, 1996; Landreth, 2002; O'Connor, 2000; Orton, 1996). Many helping professionals use play within the context of the therapeutic session to establish rapport, engage children, and provide children with a way of expressing themselves that does not rely on receptive or expressive verbal skills beyond children's developmental level. Play therapy techniques differ from traditional, verbally based strategies of counseling and therapy. In play therapy, the helping professional relies on the child's play rather than on verbal responses as the communicative medium. As Haim Ginott notes, "A child's play is his talk, and the toys are his words" (1961, p. 29). Children use play as a means of communicating their experiences (Axline, 1969; Landreth, 2002; Moustakas, 1953).

Engaging children in play therapy allows them to tell their stories and offers the therapist the opportunity to hear them. Keep in mind as you read and engage in this workbook that the concept of working in a therapeutic relationship where children are allowed to play out their feelings, thoughts, and experiences is fundamental to the play therapist, no matter what theoretical orientation the therapist adopts.

What Is a Play Therapist?

The Association for Play Therapy (www.a4pt.org) defines play therapy as "the systematic use of a theoretical model to establish an interpersonal process wherein trained play therapists use the therapeutic powers of play to help clients prevent or resolve psychosocial difficulties and achieve optimal growth and development."

We think it helps to highlight a few words and ideas that are part of this definition. Let's start with *systematic.* Our understanding of this term as it applies to play therapy means that the play therapist has a strong foundation of play therapy skills and approaches. The play therapist makes sound clinical decisions about how to employ these skills and approaches in a cohesive and thoughtful manner that is therefore systematic.

The next word that gets our attention is *trained*. The definition specifies that the helping professional be trained in play therapy. We consider training in play therapy to be a formal process that includes graduate coursework, continuing education courses, the reading of professional literature, and ongoing clinical supervision. Those of us who do this work can tell you why that is . . . it's not easy to be a play therapist. We want you to be a stellar professional play therapist: It takes a lot of training.

The term *play* also has a prominent place in this definition. Play is always a part of play therapy. Having a decent knowledge base about the importance of play in and outside of play therapy is imperative, as is an understanding of the connection between play and development. Play therapists need to distinguish between healthy and symptomatic play.

We also are drawn to the word *prevent* in this definition. A great deal of research demonstrates the healing powers of play and play therapy; we also want to honor the value of play in preventing some of the mental health and behavioral struggles we see in children.

Why Use This Workbook?

As you can see, there's a lot to play therapy that you must consider as you embark on your journey to become a play therapist. Play therapists are an elite group. We are confident that we are offering you some of the best tools in this workbook to help you reach your goal.

You may be using this workbook because, like so many of us who are doing play therapy, you have recognized that the skills and attitudes necessary to work with children in counseling relationships are not typically addressed in most preparation programs in the helping professions (Landreth, 2002). We hope that you will use this workbook to reinforce what you have already learned in trainings, graduate coursework, clinical supervision, and experience. This workbook is not a substitute in any way for those educational and experiential elements of your training. If this is your introduction to play therapy, welcome! Now go out and get additional training, education, supervision, and experience.

We wholeheartedly endorse the words of Kottman (1999) when she asserts, "Counselors cannot learn how to effectively conduct play therapy simply by reading books or attending a workshop or two. This approach to counseling children requires an entirely different mind-set than talk therapy" (p. 115). Effective counseling and play therapy with children requires more than learning skills, reading a book, or attending a workshop.

Can Anyone Be Trained in Play Therapy?

Any master's level helping professional can be trained in play therapy, but not just anyone can *be* a play therapist. We emphasize the word *be* because certain essential qualities are necessary to be an effective play therapist, and not every person possesses them. Most important to the process of play therapy is the therapist's way of *being*, rather than his or her way of *doing*. Skills and techniques can be taught and learned, but a way of *being* cannot. Child-centered play therapists must possess the core qualities of deep empathy, unconditional positive regard, and genuineness (Cochran, Nordling, & Cochran, 2010). We talk about empathy—the ability to feel the experience of another—later on in this workbook. It is especially challenging to be able to communicate our empathic understanding to children in a way they can understand.

Unconditional positive regard in play therapy means that the play therapist accepts the child unconditionally. It is through this acceptance that children will eventually be able to accept themselves. Think of yourself and the many roles you play in your life. When you are in different settings, with different people, it can at times mean that you feel the need to change the way you act and present yourself to feel accepted. That can be very uncomfortable and difficult! Where are you and who are you with when you are your most authentic self—when you're accepted exactly as you are? How does that *feel?* Amazing and freeing! That's how children are able to feel through the process of play therapy. They are free to be who they are born to be, complete with all the characteristics they possess.

Genuineness, or congruency, means that the play therapist is authentic and genuine in the expression of empathy. Children can spot a fake a mile away—they know when you are real and when you're not.

We would really like to add here that a love of children should be a "no-brainer" as far as an ideal therapist characteristic, but we have seen many supervisees who initially claimed that they didn't really like children flourish into amazing play therapists! In most cases, their initial hesitation is due to not really understanding children and therefore being afraid to work with them. The transformations we've witnessed have been remarkable.

Why Can Play Therapy Be Considered Cross-Cultural Counseling?

The relationship between client and counselor in play therapy shares many of the characteristics inherent in counseling relationships in general. Basic aspects of the counseling relationship—such as listening, empathy, and creating an atmosphere of trust and respect—are present in the relationship between play therapist and client. However, several aspects of the counseling relationship are unique to counseling relationships with children and especially to the play therapy relationship (Mullen, 2003b).

The most important aspect of the counseling relationship from the adult client's perspective, the aspect that dictates whether the intervention is perceived and experienced as successful, is the counselor's ability to demonstrate understanding to the client. Counselors who work with children also must demonstrate understanding in the context of the counseling relationship for the counseling to be effective. This means that the play therapist must be able to convey to a child, with and without words, that he or she understands the child's perspective. Creating a counseling relationship in which the child client feels understood may be more difficult than in a counseling relationship in which the client is an adult. When the client in the counseling relationship is a child, aspects of the relationship are altered (Erdman & Lampe, 1996; Landreth, 2002; Thompson & Rudolph, 2000; Stern & Newland, 1994), making the task of empathizing with the client more difficult. Children differ from adults developmentally, cognitively, emotionally, physically, and psychologically. These differences require counselors who work with children to have specialized knowledge. Erdman and Lampe (1996) suggest that it is also important to note that any cultural differences between counselor and client are likely to be enhanced by the differences accounted for by the assignment of status as adult or child.

Therapists and counselors who work with adults are unlikely to encounter some of the occurrences experienced weekly by play therapists, such as a child who climbs the coat rack in the waiting area or a client who spends the entire session talking about SpongeBob or a client who is significantly below the therapist's level of cognitive and abstract reasoning ability (Landreth, 2002). In addition, children are typically mandated clients in the sense that they did not request or seek out counseling services. Another person (an adult) in their life initiated the relationship. Children, for the most part, do not even know why they are in the counseling relationship (Mullen, 2003b). We will explore the idea of childhood as a distinct culture throughout this workbook and see how that impacts the therapeutic relationship between child and play therapist.

What Is the Child-Centered Approach?

Like other theoretical approaches to play therapy, child-centered play therapists use play as a therapeutic medium for working with children (Axline, 1969; Kottman, 1999; Landreth, 2002; O'Connor, 2000; Thompson & Ruldoph, 2000). Child-centered play therapy incorporates a developmental perspective for approaching and understanding children. Virginia M. Axline is credited as the founder and developer of child-centered play therapy, and here's how she defined it:

> Play therapy is based upon the fact that play is the child's natural medium for self expression. It is an opportunity which is given to the child to "play out" his feelings and problems just as, in certain types of adult therapy, an individual "talks out" his difficulties. (1947, p. 9)

Axline argued that it was the relationship between child and therapist, and not the play, that made it therapy. Child-centered play therapy is an outgrowth of Carl Rogers' person-centered theory (Rogers, 1951). Therefore, the person-centered approach and child-centered play therapy share a philosophical view. The child-centered approach is not merely a series of techniques or procedures. As we said earlier, grounded in the child-centered philosophy, it is not a way of doing therapy but a way of being. Therefore, if you do not believe in the philosophy, you cannot do child-centered play therapy.

In child-centered play therapy, the relationship is key. The process and not the procedure characterize this approach. We will not offer you a comprehensive explanation of the approach here, but we will share the major theoretical constructs.

The child-centered approach rests on the belief that children will heal, grow, and change if they are provided with an atmosphere where the prosocial aspects of self can flourish. This atmosphere is ideally created by the therapist, who relays trust and acceptance of the child, communicates accurate empathic understanding, and allows the child to move at his or her pace in a way that is valued. A cornerstone of the child-centered philosophy is that the therapist is able to facilitate understanding by attempting to view the world from the child's frame of reference and phenomenological perspective (Killough-McGuire, & McGuire, 2001). This therapy is a phenomenological and humanistic approach to helping that emphasizes the belief that people (including children) are striving toward actualizing self.

We have chosen to focus on the child-centered approach to play therapy in this workbook for several reasons. First, we believe that the child-centered play therapy approach contains the basic building blocks of quality play therapy. Being able to convey warmth, understanding, and empathy is the foundation of good relationships, both inside and outside of play therapy. Second, in our combined 30 years of experience doing play therapy, we have learned that, although the child-centered approach is basic, it is also what it takes to help children heal and grow. Although we sometimes augment our work so that it no longer strictly follows the tenets of child-centered therapy, the child-centered philosophy still guides our clinical decision making and is evident in our overall approach.

A Message for Readers Who Are Also Parents or Caregivers

Jodi writes . . .

I personally feel blessed that I learned about play therapy prior to becoming a parent. I was able to incorporate much of what I learned and believed about play therapy into my parenting style. I can tell you that although you would hear play therapy style limit-setting and time-structuring statements in my interactions with my children, you would also hear some yelling, impatience, and lack of empathy. I practice being thoughtful, empathic, and accepting with my children, but sometimes I am not. The children in my playroom are my children for 30 minutes at a time and usually no more than once a week. My children are my children forever, and therefore our relationship is different. This will be the case with you and your children as well. You must be accepting of yourself before you can accept another.

I wanted to mention this because many of my former students who were already parents when they started play therapy training have had a strong reaction to the course content and experience. Many of them have expressed overwhelming feelings of guilt and even despair. They share that they made many mistakes in raising their children. All parents make mistakes with their children, even ones trained in play therapy. I just wanted to make sure you keep in mind that no one "does parenting" (or anything else, for that matter) perfectly. Again, remember that you have to accept yourself before you can be accepting of someone else.

June writes . . .

I learned about play therapy after my children were grown, so I can relate to those of you who may have some guilty feelings about your past parenting "bloopers." There are many times when I think back to the time my husband and I were raising our children and think, "Wow—we made things a lot more difficult than they had to be!" I can see how many of the things we did or said, and strategies we used, were ineffective. I wish we would have instead tried simply to understand and accept our children rather than having our main mission be to get them to behave.

Thankfully, our children turned out to be wonderful and caring adults—in fact, one of our children is now a parent to three little girls, and an amazing parent at that! He had to have learned that somewhere! So please let yourself off the hook if you find yourself bashing your parenting. Your memories of raising your children may be negatively skewed. Try to remember the things you did well and give yourself credit for doing the best you knew how. And know that the skills you learn in child-centered play therapy will help you in all of the relationships in your life, not just in your relationships with children.

Before Starting This Workbook: A Recipe

Before you get started in this workbook, we would like you to take some time to think about the person you want to be in your relationships with children. Once you have cleared some space to focus on this, use the space provided to articulate what you need to be that version of yourself. Please write those thoughts (and feelings?) down here in the form of a recipe.

Title:

Ingredients:

Directions:

Other notes (serving or storing suggestions, possible substitutions, where to find any elusive ingredients, etc.):

PART 1

Why Empathy?

In this section of the workbook, you will be focusing on communicating empathy. In our experience supervising and teaching play therapy, we have noticed that many students have difficulty putting into words the distinction between empathy and sympathy. We think it's important to clarify that before we go any further.

Empathy and sympathy both involve responding sensitively to another person's experience. Empathy, however, is conveying to another an understanding of what it *feels* like to be inside of that person's emotional experience. Sympathy conveys concern and feeling sorry for another person, but not necessarily an understanding of what that other person is feeling. Empathy is a deeper, more active process. For example, I can convey empathy to my child client who has been in several different foster homes by feeling her sadness over the loss, her fear of attachment, and her uncertainty and confusion in not knowing what to expect next. I can relate to and *feel* what her experience is like. I convey sympathy to that same child by sharing sorrow for her and her situation, offering condolences, and possibly even helping to make her feel better and ease her pain (Clark, 2010).

Play therapists need to be able to communicate accurate empathic understanding to children. It is one thing to make empathic responses; it's another to communicate those responses accurately. Child-centered play therapists can demonstrate that they understand children, to children, through reflective responses. Reflections are valuable to mental health professionals regardless of the age of their clients. You are likely to find reflecting the feelings of children to be inherently difficult because children do not typically have a wealth of words to express their feelings and because some children are reluctant or developmentally unprepared to put words to their experiences. To correctly reflect the feelings of children, it is important to watch the child's facial expressions and body language. This will tell you more about what the child is feeling than will watching what the child is playing with. You can also learn a lot about how the child is feeling by listening to the child's breathing patterns and other bodily noises.

Sometimes you will make a reflection of feeling, and you will be wrong (we do this at least once a session). These are terrific opportunities to demonstrate being a fallible human being. In addition, children can clarify or correct you in these moments. That experience can be empowering for children as they recognize that they are indeed the experts of their own internal experiences, including how they are feeling.

Reflection of feeling takes practice. It may feel unnatural and robotic at first. We recommend if you have pets that you practice reflective responses with them. Dogs are especially good partners in this learning endeavor: "Scamper, you look excited to see me." (Jodi has cats, and although this technique works with them to some extent, she tends to make the same reflective responses over and over: "Robi, you are so sleepy right now.") Have fun with this. Being able to reflect feelings accurately will benefit you in *all* of your relationships.

Feelings Words: Translations for Children

So here's your first assignment! What we would like you to do is attempt to create multiple ways of reflecting each feelings word listed to a young child. Do not limit yourself to words. Facial expressions, large or small gestures, sound effects, and interjections are all acceptable. It helps to pair words and facial expressions, gestures, sound effects, or interjections for the most comprehensive communication. You may want to know that the more "schooled" you are, the harder this assignment will be because it asks you to simplify your communication to meet the developmental level of children.

Your Turn: Translating Feelings Words

For each of the following words, reflect the meaning in a child-friendly way. Sample answers appear on page 105.

1. Annoyed _____

2. Ashamed _____

3. Bored _____

4. Brave _____

5. Cooperative _____

6. Curious _____

7. Defective _____

8. Disappointed _____

9. Disconnected _____

10. Enthusiastic _____

11. Frustrated _____

12. Hopeless _____

13. Insecure _____

14. Malicious _____

15. Obstinate _____

16. Overwhelmed _____

17. Satisfied _____

18. Tentative _____

19. Unpopular _____

20. Vulnerable _____

Your Turn: Identifying Feelings

Here are several pictures of children. You have no context and no verbalizations. Reflect how the child is feeling based only on his or her facial expression. (Try to come up with three or more possible feelings for each picture.)

Possible feelings:

Possible feelings:

Possible feelings:

Possible feelings:

Possible feelings:

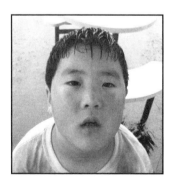

Possible feelings:

Reflecting Feelings

Reflection of feelings is a basic counseling skill. It is also a basic skill in play therapy. It is crucial that the child-centered play therapist be able to reflect the feelings of children. Reflecting feelings in children can be difficult because children are unlikely to express their feelings verbally. It will take keen observation skills, including paying close attention to the child's face, to discern feelings and make a reflective response. It is through this skill that child-centered play therapists demonstrate to children that they understand. Reflective listening also allows the play therapist to demonstrate accurate empathic understanding. An adequate number and variety of reflective responses are necessary to help children become aware of their emotions. It is this awareness of emotions that leads to the appropriate acceptance and expression of emotions (Ray, 2004).

Here are some examples of reflections of feeling:

- You are feeling frustrated.

- That was scary to you.

- You feel safe enough to try.

Your Turn: Reflecting Feelings

For the following responses, please check each response that is a reflection of feeling. If it is, replace the feelings word with another feelings word. (We want you to grow your feelings vocabulary.)

EXAMPLE: You were worried.   ☑ *You were concerned.*

If it is not a reflective response, do not check it. Instead, try to change it into one.

EXAMPLE: You built a tower.   ☐ *You feel proud of that tower.*

There are many possible answers. Some options appear on page 107.

1. You were very scared.   ☐ _____

   _____

2. You want that toy.   ☐ _____

   _____

3. That was surprising. □ _____

   _____

4. You are so tired. □ _____

   _____

5. You are sad. □ _____

   _____

6. That was a good one. □ _____

   _____

7. That shocked you. □ _____

   _____

8. You feel like a superhero. □ _____

   _____

9. You are angry. □ _____

   _____

10. That was frustrating. □ _____

   _____

Empathizing Versus Giving Solutions

Sometimes, we give solutions instead of offering empathy. Unfortunately, giving solutions denies or minimizes the child's feelings instead of capturing them. It is natural to want children to feel better and not feel hurt, so reflecting hurt and sad feelings is not easy. In the following example, imagine that a child is crying because he spilled his milk and got reprimanded. An empathic statement would be "You're so upset and feel really sad that Daddy scolded you." This is not making it all better for the child, but it is responding with what the child is feeling at the moment. It allows the child to feel understood and validated, even if it doesn't change what happened. Saying to the child, "Don't cry" does not convey understanding.

Imagine yourself in a similar situation: You get home from a day of work in which everything that could go wrong did go wrong. You're sad and worn out, and at the sight of your significant other, you start to cry. Now imagine how you would feel if your significant other said, "Don't cry—tomorrow's another day." Now imagine how you would feel if your significant other instead said, "You're really upset and sad. It was an awful day for you." I'm sure you will agree that it would feel different (and better) if you were greeted with an empathic statement, even if it didn't change the rotten day you had!

"Solution statements" are often offered to children to make them stop hurting so that the adults in their lives can feel better. These statements attempt to smooth things over or make them better but do not convey empathy to the child.

Your Turn: Making Empathic Statements

Change the solution statement to an empathic statement. Some sample answers appear on page 108.

    EXAMPLE: Don't cry.   <u>*You're so upset.*</u>

1. Don't worry.   _____

                               _____

2. It will be okay.   _____

                               _____

3. It's not a big deal.   _____

                               _____

4. You can't win them all.

   _____

   _____

5. That's life.

   _____

   _____

6. It could be worse.

   _____

   _____

7. You'll do fine.

   _____

   _____

8. Everything will be all right.

   _____

   _____

9. It's not that important.

   _____

   _____

10. You'll get another chance.

   _____

   _____

11. Some problems solve themselves.

   _____

   _____

13. There's always a bright side.

   _____

   _____

14. People grow from experiences like this.

   _____

   _____

15. It's for your own good.

   _____

   _____

PART 2

The Child-Centered Approach

In this section, you will find exercises and discussion designed to ground you in the child-centered approach. We will spend some time comparing child-centered play therapy to other approaches, addressing the Eight Basic Principles, and discussing how the child-centered play therapy approach is enhanced by viewing childhood as a culture.

Child-Centered Play Therapy Versus Other Approaches

The relationship between the child and the play therapist is cornerstone of the child's growth. The philosophy is as important (if not more) than any one particular skill. The following table, based on the work of Landreth (2002), summarizes the basic tenets of child-centered play therapy in relation to other therapeutic approaches.

Child-Centered Approach	Other Approaches	Discussion
Here and now	There and then	In child-centered play therapy, what is happening in the moment is what is important. What has happened in the past and what will happen in the future is not the focus of the intervention. The temporal focus is the present.
Developmental	Remedial	Child-centered play therapists believe in a growth model. People, including children, grow, so trying to remediate and change them is not part of the approach; facilitating growth and development is.
Person	Problem	The child is the center of the child-centered play therapy intervention and not the diagnosis, behavior, or academic or social problem.
Affect	Cognition and behavior	Child-centered play therapists focus on how children feel and aspire to accurately communicate empathic understanding.
Understanding	Explaining	For child-centered play therapists, understanding the phenomenological perspective of the child is far more important than being able to explain the child's behaviors.
Accepting	Correcting	In child-centered play therapy, the therapist accepts the child exactly as he or she is. It is not the job of the play therapist to take a corrective stance in the relationship with the child.
Therapist as a person	Therapist as an expert	The child-centered play therapist is a fallible human being and genuine adult in the child's life. The play therapist is not the expert on the child; the child is.
Spontaneity	Structure	The child is the director of the session, so child-centered play therapy sessions are structured by the child. The playroom toys used and/or the activities engaged in are chosen by the child.

Child-Centered Approach	Other Approaches	Discussion
Action	Talk	The child communicates through play, so talk, although a viable means of communication, is not necessary.
Attitude change	Behavior change	Child-centered play therapists believe that attitude change is the most salient and significant form of change. Observable changes will come after attitude change.
Child's direction	Therapist's instruction	The child directs and takes responsibility for the content of the session. The child-centered play therapist keeps the space safe and does not direct the child's play in any subtle or obvious manner.
Child's wisdom	Therapist's knowledge	Child-centered play therapists regard each child as the expert of his or her own experience. The culture of childhood is respected and valued. Child-centered play therapists have a great deal to learn from their clients.

Your Turn: Is It Child Centered?

Here are some simple exchanges between client and play therapist. Your job is to decide whether the play therapist's response is child-centered. Sample answers and explanations appear on page 109.

1. Client: (Looks around the playroom and finds an action figure he played with last session.)

   Therapist: You played with that last time, too.

   ☐ **Child centered** ☐ **NOT**

2. Client: (Picks up a feather boa, then looks frightened and throws it.) Ahhhhh!!! I don't like that!

   Therapist: You're really scared. Look, it's just a feather boa—it can't hurt you.

   ☐ **Child centered** ☐ **NOT**

3. Client: (Tries to shoot a basket several times and misses. Looks sad and stops trying.)

   Therapist: You almost got it that time—try again.

   ☐ **Child centered** ☐ **NOT**

4. Client: (On hearing that playtime is over.) I didn't get a chance to play with that!

   Therapist: You can play with that next time if you want.

   ☐ **Child centered** ☐ **NOT**

5. Client: (Gets to second level of a limit, but does not reach the limit where she will be asked to leave the session.)

   Therapist: You're making good choices in here.

   ☐ **Child centered** ☐ **NOT**

6. Client: (Gets out the doctor kit and looks the pieces over, inspecting each one.)

   Therapist: It looks like you want to check me out.

   ☐ **Child centered** ☐ **NOT**

7. Client: Here's some for you and some for me. Let's eat.

   Therapist: You like to share with me.

   ☐ **Child centered** ☐ **NOT**

8. Client: (Struggles with tape while making something.) This stupid tape isn't working.

   Therapist: Here—it looks like a stapler would do the job better.

   ☐ **Child centered** ☐ **NOT**

The Child-Centered Approach

9. Client: How do you spell *school?*

    Therapist: You want to know how to spell it: S-C-H-O-O-L.

    ☐ **Child centered**   ☐ **NOT**

10. Client: I made this delicious soup for you. It has worms in it.

    Therapist: That's crazy. What kind of soup has worms in it?

    ☐ **Child centered**   ☐ **NOT**

11. Client: I wish you were my mommy.

    Therapist: I can't be your mommy, but I can be your friend.

    ☐ **Child centered**   ☐ **NOT**

12. Client: Hurry up and get me that basketball over there.

    Therapist: You like being able to tell me what to do.

    ☐ **Child centered**   ☐ **NOT**

13. Client: (Playing with figures in dollhouse) This boy is scared—he's hiding in the closet.

    Therapist: You're afraid.

    ☐ **Child centered**   ☐ **NOT**

14. Client: (Using a male adult figure from the dollhouse) He's mad, so he's hitting the baby.

    Therapist: He's scary—just like your dad.

    ☐ **Child centered**   ☐ **NOT**

15. Client: (Looking closely at the dollhouse figures) Which one is supposed to be the mom?

    Therapist: Hmm . . . let's see. Which one looks like the mom to you?

    ☐ **Child centered**   ☐ **NOT**

16. Client: Aren't you supposed to be asking me questions?

    Therapist: You're confused—this is different from what you thought.

    ☐ **Child centered**   ☐ **NOT**

17. Client: Do you have any pink Play-Doh? I don't like this color.

    Therapist: I might—let me check. You don't like blue.

    ☐ **Child centered**   ☐ **NOT**

18. Client: I don't know what to play with.

   Therapist: There are lots of things in here for you to do.

   ☐ **Child centered**   ☐ **NOT**

19. Client: I don't like these toys—they're stupid.

   Therapist: You don't like any of these things.

   ☐ **Child centered**   ☐ **NOT**

20. Client: How much time is left? I'm not done.

   Therapist: You're concerned you won't be able to finish in time.

   ☐ **Child centered**   ☐ **NOT**

21. Client: Do other kids play in this room, too?

   Therapist: Yes, we have lots of kids that come here to play.

   ☐ **Child centered**   ☐ **NOT**

22. Client: When am I going to see you next?

   Therapist: You will see me next week.

   ☐ **Child centered**   ☐ **NOT**

23. Client: Can you open this for me?

   Therapist: You think that's difficult and would like my help.

   ☐ **Child centered**   ☐ **NOT**

The Eight Basic Principles

The basic principles that guide the child-centered play therapist are very simple, but they are incredibly powerful in their possibilities when followed sincerely, consistently, and intelligently by the play therapist. The principles, originally proposed by Virginia Axline (1969), are as follows:

1. The play therapist must create a warm and friendly relationship with the child. Good rapport is established as soon as possible.

2. The play therapist accepts the child exactly as he or she is.

3. The play therapist establishes a feeling of permissiveness in the relationship so that the child feels free to express his or her feelings.

4. The play therapist recognizes the feelings the child is expressing and reflects those feelings back to the child in such a way that the child gains insight into his or her behavior.

5. The play therapist has a strong respect for the child's ability to solve his or her own problems if given an opportunity to do so. The responsibility to make choices and to change is the child's.

6. The play therapist does not attempt to direct the child's behaviors or verbalizations in any way. The child leads the way, and the play therapist follows.

7. The play therapist does not attempt to hurry the child along. Play therapy is a gradual process and is honored as such by the play therapist.

8. The play therapist establishes only those limitations that are necessary to ground the child to the world of reality and to make the child aware of his or her responsibility in the relationship.

These principles may seem simple, but they require you to live the philosophy of the child-centered approach. Techniques are important, but the "why" behind the techniques is fundamental. Think of it this way: In play therapy, it's not what you *do* that makes it therapy, but who you *are*. We want you to have a solid foundation for connecting with children in a therapeutic way. The purpose of the next exercise is to have you focus on the philosophy and who you are as a play therapist.

Your Turn: Living the Principles

Refer to the Eight Basic Principles and answer the following questions accordingly.

1. Review each principle. How do you implement the Eight Basic Principles in your current interactions with children?

   - Are there any that you don't implement?

   - What gets in your way?

   - How could you implement the principles?

   _____

   _____

   _____

2. Review each principle. Do you implement any of them in your everyday life?

   - If yes, which ones, and how?

   - If no, what gets in your way?

   - How would it impact your relationships if you did follow the principles?

   - Will you begin to incorporate one of the eight principles in your everyday life?

   _____

   _____

   _____

3. Review each principle. Which of them would be least difficult for you to follow? Why?

   _____

   _____

4. Review each principle. Which of them would be most difficult for you to follow? Why?

   _____

   _____

5. Review each principle. Which of the principles do you need the people in your life to follow to feel more supported? How can you communicate this?

_____

_____

6. Review the principles. Think about your childhood. Is there someone who seemed to follow these principles in his or her interactions with you?

   - If yes, what was that like?

   - If no, what do you imagine would have been different if someone had?

_____

_____

_____

7. Communicate the Eight Basic Principles philosophy to someone who supports your work. What is/was it like to talk about it?

_____

_____

_____

Childhood as Culture

To be truly effective as a play therapist, it is essential to view childhood as a distinct culture. When providing counseling to children, we have an ethical responsibility to become familiar with the elements of their culture. To do this, we first need to define *culture*. Culture is what makes one group of people unique from other groups and includes language, customs, rules, beliefs, values, and behaviors.

At this point, we'd like you to think back to your childhood: Are there songs you remember singing and games you remember playing with your friends on the playground? Most likely, it was the children who knew the rules of the games and the words to the songs, not the adults. This is because the games and songs were part of child culture and not the dominant adult culture. Did you share certain beliefs and superstitions with your friends that were restricted to the child population? Did you ever make a "pinky promise" with a friend? Were you ever convinced that if you "stepped on a crack, you'd break your mother's back" or that if you didn't hold your breath going past a cemetery horrible things would happen? These are a few simple examples that support the view of childhood as a separate culture.

Your Turn: Childhood as Culture

Next described are several elements that characterize culture and subculture and the ways they are constructed. This is a complex perspective. Take your time reading and responding to the following items. Some sample responses are given below each question.

Rules

Rules are the cultural components that guide conduct and actions.

1. What are two rules specific to the culture of childhood?

   _____

   _____

In adulthood, rules are covert, whereas in childhood, they are likely to be explicitly stated. How about the five-second rule? (If it's on the floor for less than five seconds, you can still eat it.) Clearly, that originated in the culture of childhood! Here are some other examples:

- Possession is the law. If you have it in your hand, it is yours.

- Finders keepers, losers weepers. (This is similar to the first example in that if an item is in your possession, it belongs to you.)

- Utensils for eating your food are optional.

Values

Values are ideas that do not require external proof to be considered true. Values define the boundaries of culture by aiding in communication because they are shared among group members. Values are often sources of disagreement between cultural groups because each group experiences the situation from its own perspective (Pederson & Ivey, 1993).

2. Identify two values that are shared among people whose cultural affiliation is childhood.

   _____

   _____

Pederson and Ivey (1993) offer the example of homework in demonstrating different values and how they can be a source of conflict between children and adults. Children may experience homework from a short-term perspective and as taking away from free time. Parents (members of the culture of adulthood) view homework differently, through a long-term lens, where the benefits are worth the short-term loss.

In the culture of childhood, the perception of time has a great deal to do with values. Because the temporal focus of children is the present, their values will represent this perspective. What do adults mean when they say "too long" to a child, and how would the child know what the adult would consider an appropriate amount of time?

Think of the potential disagreements between the cultural groups of adulthood and childhood with regard to these adult statements:

- Hurry up—we only have three minutes.

- You are taking too long.

- Just a few more minutes.

Children are usually at the mercy of adult schedules. What happens typically when an adult says, "Just a few more minutes" to a child?

_____

_____

Children will attempt to hold adults to their word. When a few minutes is up, the child expects the adult will follow through. How would this exchange impact the adult-child relationship if the adult repeatedly does not follow through with what he or she said?

_____

_____

Customs

Customs are also elements of culture. They are best described as longstanding practices or conventions that regulate social life.

4. Can you name three customs practiced in the culture of childhood?

_____

_____

_____

Many childhood games could be considered a matter of custom. Selection of teams through "One potato, two potato . . ." or "Rock, paper, scissors" are examples.

Language

Language comprises the various communicative mediums present in the culture.

5. What are some communications that are specific to the culture of childhood?

_____

_____

_____

It is a perfectly acceptable practice to make up words in the culture of childhood, although this is not the case in adulthood. At four, Jodi's daughter was trying to communicate to her father and mother that she was annoyed and felt the situation she was in was unfair. Jodi writes:

> She turned to us and said, "I just think this whole thing is *impurtutious.*" In that moment, we were able to speak her cultural language and demonstrate that we understood her plight by reflecting her feelings, although neither of us had heard this word uttered before. We did not correct her as adults typically do.

Another example that stands out among children is the ability of older children to understand the language of younger children, to which adults are not privy.

Status

The cultural component of status speaks to the value of members in the culture, particularly in contrast to the dominant culture.

6. How is status determined within the culture of childhood? Write down two examples.

_____

_____

Size matters, and children who are taller and/or look older (more like members of the dominant culture) may have higher status within the culture of childhood. Status also comes with knowledge of the dominant culture. Children who know about, or have experiences with, elements of adolescent or adult cultures achieve higher status in their own culture. Status is also established in the culture of childhood by challenges and comparisons. Were you ever "double-dog dared" as a child or adolescent? Having a contemporary double-dog dare you is serious business in the culture of childhood—your response could be your only chance to increase your credibility with your peers.

View of Dominant Culture: Adulthood

If childhood is a subculture, then the dominant culture is the culture of adulthood. It is reasonable to believe that a shared view of dominant culture exists.

7. Name three separate perspectives held by members of the culture of childhood about members of the culture of adulthood.

_____

_____

_____

Adults have different rules for children than they do for members of their own culture. Adults can lie, and there are no consequences. The examples of the tooth fairy, Santa Claus, and the bogeyman bear out this assertion.

Adults also believe they know best about the internal states of children. This belief leads to such utterances as "How can you be hungry? You just ate" or "Put your jacket on. I'm cold." Here's an example: Jodi's son Andrew eats macaroni and cheese sandwiches. His cultural counterparts think this brilliant. Those of us in adulthood may actually agree but would not likely want others to know that this is what we are eating for lunch.

Another reason it is an awesome responsibility (and honor) to be a play therapist: Skilled play therapists are able to navigate the cultural barriers between adulthood and childhood. Play therapists should anticipate a more complex role in their relationships with children because they have this added responsibility to serve as translators between the two cultures (Mullen, 2003b).

Blending the Culture of Childhood and the Eight Basic Principles

Listed here are the Eight Basic Principles (yes, again, because we want you to become well-acquainted with them). For each principle, we will discuss how viewing childhood as a distinct culture factors into practical application. We have given an example of what each principle might look like in a session.

Your Turn: Blending Culture and Principles

As you are thinking about the Eight Basic Principles and the culture of childhood, try to formulate your own examples from your clinical, personal, or professional experiences.

1. The play therapist must create a warm and friendly relationship with the child. Good rapport is established as soon as possible.

When we work with children, we are aware of the cross-cultural relationship. We are representatives from the culture of adulthood. In order to develop a relationship quickly with a child, we must be able to traverse cultural barriers and present ourselves in a way that demonstrates that we honor the culture of childhood. The fastest, most effective way to do this is to meet the child at his or her physical level. Therefore, when we greet our clients we make sure to crouch down so we can be at child level. In addition, children are incredible readers of nonverbal language. When we meet with a child, we smile warmly.

> Parent: Say hello to Dr. Jodi. She is going to help you.
>
> Jodi: (Crouching down to the child's level, smiling, and speaking to the child.) Hi, Sammy, let's spend some time playing today. You can call me Jodi. Mom, we will see you in a little while after Sammy and I have played.

Your example:

_____

_____

_____

2. The play therapist accepts the child exactly as he or she is.

Our adult cultural counterparts often communicate to children that they are not okay. In child-centered play therapy, it is important to communicate that children are okay just the way they are. None of us wants to be defined by our behaviors—that is something our two cultures have in common. Because children are part of a marginalized culture, children's perspectives, thoughts, feelings, and behaviors are often minimized or denied by the dominant adult culture, therefore communicating that people from their culture (childhood) are not accepted. For example, if a child says, "I hate my sister," rather than demonstrate that we accept how the child is feeling about her sister in the moment, we correct: "You don't hate your sister." Consequently, we have just implied this: "I know more about how you are feeling than you do, AND I do not accept how you are feeling."

> Child: I hate you. I don't want to stay in your stupid playroom.

> June: You are really mad at me right now and want me to know what it's like to have hurt feelings.

Your example:

_____

_____

_____

3. The play therapist establishes a feeling of permissiveness in the relationship so that the child feels free to express his or her feelings.

From the perspective of the culture of childhood, our culture of adulthood must seem very restrictive. There are rules and structure in many interactions between our two cultures. Seldom does the representative from the culture of childhood have any say in the negotiation of these implicit and explicit relational rules. Therefore, children's perspectives and experiences are not given the space to emerge and be shared when our two cultures engage in relationships.

> Jodi: Jessie, this is a very special room. You can do almost anything in this room. If there is something you cannot do, I will tell you. You can also say anything."

> Child: If I say a bad word, you won't like me.

> Jodi: It's hard for you to trust what I am saying. Jessie, you can say anything in this room.

Your example:

_____

_____

_____

4. The play therapist recognizes the feelings the child is expressing and reflects those feelings back to the child in such a way that the child gains insight into his or her behavior.

Too often, children's feelings are minimized or denied by even caring and thoughtful people whose primary cultural identification is that of adulthood. When we deny and minimize the feelings of children, they likely feel that we do not understand or, even worse, do not care. Here's a classic example: A child falls and scrapes his knee. The child is crying and the adult responds, "You're okay—that wasn't so bad." What if the adult recognized and honored the child's feelings? Maybe then the reply would go something like this: "You fell down, and that hurt."

Child: It's not fair that I can't stay longer.

June: You feel mad and disappointed that our time is up.

Your example:

_____

_____

_____

5. The play therapist has a strong respect for the child's ability to solve his or her own problems if given an opportunity to do so. The responsibility to make choices and to change is the child's.

In our culture of adulthood, it seems that we can never move fast enough. When we are interacting with people from the culture of childhood, we often forget that in their culture things are not so rushed. There's a physical component to this, too. Just watch the dynamics when a child and adult are out walking. Children can only walk so fast, and the stride of a preschooler is likely to be a third of the stride of an adult. We rush children in so many circumstances, particularly in situations where there are problem-solving opportunities. However, if we always solve children's problems for them, they will have little experience with or tolerance for frustration. As children grow, they become accustomed to having their problems solved for them. In addition, they will be unfamiliar with the feeling of pride when they recognize they are capable.

>Child: I can't open this.

>Jodi: It is so frustrating.

>Child: I hate this thing.

>Jodi: You got really mad and decided not to keep trying.

Your example:

_____

_____

_____

6. The play therapist does not attempt to direct the child's behaviors or verbalizations in any way. The child leads the way, and the play therapist follows.

In child-centered play therapy, the child gets to make the decisions and lead the way. Children do not have much experience with this dynamic in the context of a relationship with an adult. Some children will be suspicious, others will test it out, and still others will be scared and/or perplexed and look for your direction. In fact, children are often confused when they are in a relationship with an adult and the adult does not set the agenda or direct their play.

A quick story: A seven-year-old girl that Jodi had been seeing in play therapy for almost six months started off tentatively in the playroom. Jodi reflected often to her in those early sessions that she was feeling unsure about me, the room, and herself. After much testing and just as much consistency, the girl realized that Jodi was truly going to let her run the show. She created a role-play scenario, directing Jodi to be a witch. She was the princess. Shortly after the role-play began—she in her princess crown and Jodi in her witch's hat—she turned and said, "Okay, now I need you to pretend you are a grown up." Recognizing that she had truly crossed the line into the culture of childhood, Jodi responded, "I bet I can do that."

>Child: I don't know what to do. What should I do?

>June: You feel pressured to decide.

>Child: Yeah, just tell me—pick something.

June: It's strange when adults don't tell you what to do.

Child: Can't you just be the boss and tell me?

June: Mandy, in this room you can choose to do almost anything.

Your example:

_____

_____

_____

7. The play therapist does not attempt to hurry the child along. Play therapy is a gradual process and is honored as such by the play therapist.

As stated earlier, the culture of childhood does not share the same conceptualization of time as the culture of adulthood. The child-centered philosophy is consistent with the notion that therapy—just like growth, healing, and change—happens gradually. Many adults would like you to "fix" the children with whom you are working, and there seems to be an arbitrary time in which that "fixing" is supposed to happen. The notion of fixing is inconsistent with the child-centered philosophy, as is the notion of time constraints. Of course, practical time constraints do exist, but you cannot rush the process of therapy. Because you are a genuinely helpful and caring person, you may feel as though you can speed progress in children along. However, when you do that, you are not respecting the notion of time (and certainly development) in the culture of childhood.

Another quick illustration: Before she became a vegan, Jodi's favorite meal was roast turkey. She and her family would eat turkey only on holidays because it takes a long time to cook. It's possible to microwave a turkey, and it will indeed be cooked and cooked quickly. However, Jodi wouldn't want to eat one cooked this way. Would you?

Child: (Enters and stands in the middle of the playroom.)

Therapist: You look like you don't feel like playing.

Child: (Nods affirmatively.)

Therapist: You are going to take your time in here.

Child: (Nods affirmatively.)

Your example:

_____

_____

_____

8. The play therapist establishes only those limitations that are necessary to ground the child to the world of reality and to make the child aware of his or her responsibility in the relationship.

Children must think we adults are very hypocritical people. Our culture possesses very different rules for the members of our culture than it does for members of the culture of childhood. For instance, in our culture it is okay to lie and say, "No, you don't look fat." Yet if children lie while interacting with adults, it is a punishable offense. Adults are inconsistent in their interactions with children. Children need us to be consistent and help them contain their emotions when they are feeling out of control.

Limit setting allows us to provide that level of support without imposing what must seem to children like arbitrary rules. In the therapeutic playroom, limits are set to help children stay safe, to help the therapist remain safe, and to maintain the safety of the physical setting. Limits are set so children can make decisions about their behavior on the basis of their knowledge of consequences and other choices they can make. When you use limit-setting skills in the playroom, the child learns that you mean what you say. If you set only necessary limits, the child is likely to respect your rules because by setting only necessary limits you demonstrate your respect for the child. The child subsequently learns that you will indeed be there, even when the child makes poor choices with regard to safety, and that your relationship is strong enough to withstand mistakes. Limit setting is the most difficult skill in child-centered play therapy. Expect that learning the skill will take a great deal of practice. (We'll talk more about limit setting later, in Part 3 of the workbook.)

> Child: (Pulls the therapist's hair.)
>
> Therapist: Lyla, remember I told you there are some things you cannot do in here. You cannot pull my hair. You wanted me to feel hurt. You can pull the doll's hair.
>
> Child: (Pulls the therapist's hair again.)

The Child-Centered Approach   **39**

Therapist: Lyla, you are so mad, and you want to hurt me. You cannot pull my hair, and if you do it again our time will be up for today. You can choose to pretend to pull my hair, and I'll act like it hurts bad.

Your example:

_____

_____

_____

PART 3

Skills and Guidelines

This is the section where you will find examples, exercises, and commentary designed to structure your experience in the playroom. We will give explicit instructions and lay out a clear format for play therapy sessions. When you are just starting out on this journey, you should stick closely to the instructions and scripts provided. If you do, you will find it easier to manage the nuances that develop in the playroom as you integrate the philosophy and the approach. Later, when you have more training, supervision, and experience, you can put your own unique spin on what you say and do within the framework of child-centered play therapy.

Tracking

Tracking is a very useful skill in the play therapy session. It is a simple response consisting of verbal documentation of what the play therapist is observing. Simply stated, a tracking response *tracks* the behaviors of the child in the play therapy session. By tracking the child's behavior, the play therapist proves to the child that the play therapist is attentive and accepting. According to Ray (2004), tracking responses also serve to immerse the play therapist in the child's world and experience. This skill is critical to the play therapy process and is the most basic skill used in the playroom. Tracking responses need to be balanced with higher level play therapy skills such as reflection of feeling, as discussed in Part 1 of the workbook.

Your Turn: Making Tracking Responses

Here are some behaviors frequently displayed in a play therapy session. In the space provided, make a tracking response. Sample tracking responses can be found on page 114.

EXAMPLE:

Child picks up baby bottle and looks at it.   <u>You wanted to check that out.</u>

1. Child stands on the chair.   _____

    _____

2. Child jumps up and down.   _____

    _____

3. Child uses toy food to "feed" the baby doll.   _____

    _____

4. Child tries several crayons.   _____

    _____

5. Child looks out the window after hearing a sudden noise.   _____

    _____

Responding to Children's Questions

Children will be very curious about you, the play therapy process, the playroom, and the toys. You can anticipate that they will, therefore, ask you questions. Some children use question asking to form or, conversely, to avoid relationships. In child-centered play therapy, grounded in the philosophy and Eight Basic Principles, it is best to try and reflect the child's feeling when asked a question. Usually, if you use a reflection to respond to the question, you have met the child's need, and he or she will move on. Sometimes the child persists and asks again. Try reflecting again. In the event that this does not work and the question is an answerable question, then answer the question. It has been our experience that once we answer one question, the child asks many more. These questions seem to get in the way of our relationship with the child.

Here's an example of what typically happens when you use reflection (the child moves on):

> Child: What's this toy?
>
> Therapist: You are wondering what that's supposed to be.
>
> Child: It's a boat.
>
> Therapist: You are confident you know what it is.

With a more persistent child, the exchange might look like this:

> Child: How much more time is left?
>
> Therapist: You are worried we are running out of time.
>
> Child: Yes, how much time is left?
>
> Therapist: You would feel more comfortable if you knew how much time was left.
>
> Child: Yeah.

With an even more persistent child:

> Child: How old are you?
>
> Therapist: You are wondering about me.
>
> Child: Yeah, how old are you?
>
> Therapist: You are very curious.

Child: Just tell me.

Therapist: Thirty-six.

Several years ago Jodi worked with a 12-year-old boy named Chris who had a developmental delay. Chris responded very well to the child-centered play therapy approach. However, Chris would ask many questions during the session. Jodi gathered that this was his way of demonstrating that he cared about her. A typical exchange would go something like this:

Chris: How old are you?

Jodi: You are curious about me.

Chris: Do you have kids?

Jodi: You are wondering what I do when I am not in here with you.

Chris: What did you eat for dinner last night?

Jodi: You want to tell me about what you like to eat.

This could go on for the entire session. The incessant question asking did not stand in the way of Chris's play, so Jodi was usually able to break up the responses to his questions with therapeutic responses gleaned from his play and facial expressions. One day, Jodi decided to see what would happen if she just answered. She had known Chris long enough to suspect that he would not stick with the same question she reflected and would simply pick another question. Here's what happened:

Chris: What's your dad's name?

Jodi: Marty.

Chris: Tell him I say hi!

And that was it. No more questions for the entire session!

Your Turn: Responding to Questions

The following are all questions we have been asked. Please respond to each query with a reflection, as described n the preceding discussion. See page 114 for sample answers.

1. What time is it?   _____

          _____

2. Do other kids come here?
     _____

     _____

3. Do you have kids?
     _____

     _____

4. What's this toy called?
     _____

     _____

5. Why do you talk like that?
     _____

     _____

6. Can I swear in here?
     _____

     _____

7. Can I stay more minutes?
     _____

     _____

8. Why can't I spank you?
     _____

     _____

9. Do you love me?
     _____

     _____

10. Can I leave now?
     _____

     _____

The following are "challenge questions." We have been asked each and every one of these.

11. Are you a boy or a girl?
     _____

     _____

12. How come you're so fat?
     _____

     _____

13. Would you like to see my penis? _____

_____

14. Your breath smells—what did you eat for lunch? _____

_____

15. Do you want to smell my fart? _____

_____

Responding to Children's Directions

In the child-centered play therapy session, children lead the way. Essentially, that means they get to direct the play, be the boss, and even direct you. It is unusual for us as adults to respond to the commands of children. A sociocultural pecking order exists that emphasizes that adults are in charge and children have little power and control. As VanFleet, Sywulak, and Caparosa (2010) state, "It is important to remember that children are quite used to adults' taking the lead outside of play therapy sessions, and may not quite trust the permissive atmosphere that the therapist has established" (p. 34). The stereotypical adult response to a child's asking why he or she has do what an adult says is a fine example: "Because I said so, that's why!"

The power and control dynamic that typically exists in child-adult relationships is very different in the therapeutic playroom. Children are told from the beginning that this is a *special* room and that they *can do almost anything*. Those are power-enhancing directives. Some children will respond to that sense of power by being not only the director of themselves and of the play, but also of you.

When a child in a play therapy session directs or orders you do to something, you can handle the situation in several ways. Some ways are certainly more therapeutic than others. The most important thing is not what you do, but what you don't do. Do not take the child's bossing you around personally. The child is merely experimenting with a sense of power and control. Because children don't often have a lot of experience having significant or even equal power in child-adult relationships, the way they use their power lacks finesse.

What you can do in response to a child's directive is generally one of two things: You can either continue to follow the child's lead or return the responsibility to the child. By following the child's lead, you simply do as the child says (within reason, for safety). This is usually a good response choice during a role-play.

Returning responsibility to the child is a way of responding that acknowledges that you understand what the child is saying and that you believe in the child enough for the child to do whatever it is. Here's an example:

> Child: Go get me that sword.
>
> Therapist: You are very serious. You want me to get that, even though you could get that sword for yourself.

This second type of response is more complex because it requires you to do a quick assessment. Does the child need to experience the sense of power over you more than the sense of personal capability? Once you decide, that assessment dictates which response you use. In addition, the response can be strengthened if a reflection of feeling is also embedded in the response. In the preceding example, the therapist notes that the child is very serious.

Your Turn: Responding to Directions

Let's have you give it a try. Please read the order or direction from the child in the example. Decide if you should follow the child's lead or return the responsibility, then give a response accordingly. We'll give you our suggestions on page 115.

1. Shut the lights, NOW! _____

   _____

2. You close your eyes. _____

   _____

3. Please get me some more paper. _____

   _____

4. Tell me I'm pretty. _____

   _____

5. Pretend to eat this apple. _____

   _____

6. Give me that paint brush. _____

   _____

7. Tie my shoe. _____

   _____

8. Go sit in the corner. _____

   _____

9. Zip your mouth shut—no
   more talking! _____

   _____

10. Go over there and get me
    that truck.

    _____

    _____

Setting Limits

Limits in play therapy are rules or guidelines for behavior. They are explicitly defined and enforced by imposing consequences or results if the rules are broken. The rationale for setting limits in child-centered play therapy is grounded in the belief that children need help to define their boundaries and feel safe while simultaneously being able to explore their environment and try out behaviors. Setting limits in child-centered play therapy allows children to learn that what happens to them is a direct consequence of their behavior. They can begin to take responsibility for their actions through proper limit setting and consequences.

Most children are familiar with the rules and restrictions that are usually presented to them at the beginning of a situation—for example, "Claire, before you go in the back yard, remember, there is no throwing sand and no going down the slide backward." In many cases, the rules presented may be necessary. But Claire may not even have thought about going down the slide backward or throwing sand! Limits in play therapy are similar to rules, but a main difference is that they are not presented to the child unless they are needed. This gives the child the freedom to explore without restrictions.

Consider these factors before making a limit:

- Is this limit necessary for the safety of the child?

- Is this limit necessary for my safety?

- Is this limit necessary for the protection of property?

- Is this limit enforceable?

Why set as few limits as possible? Here are some very compelling reasons:

- Children cannot be expected to remember many rules.

- If only necessary boundaries are imposed, the child can explore the situation and can truly lead the way.

- Because consistency is important (and you want to be viewed as a person who means what he or she says), the fewer the limits imposed, the more likely it is that you will enforce them every time they are broken.

Steps in Setting Limits

Step 1: Determine whether a limit is necessary

Here are some examples of limits in the playroom:

- Nothing should be thrown at the mirrors, videocamera, or windows.

- No hurting the play therapist or self (child).

- No sharp objects should be directed at the bop bag.

- The room should not be left during the session except for one trip to the bathroom.

It's critical that children stay in the playroom so they can engage in the therapeutic process and remain physically safe and so confidentiality can be maintained. It is likely that children will need to leave the play therapy room to use the bathroom. Bathroom breaks can be handled by stating the limit as needed.

> Therapist: You can only leave this special room when you want to go to the bathroom. We can leave now.

When the child reenters the room, you can reintroduce the child to the situation:

> Therapist: We are in the special room again.

Tip: The bathroom trip can be avoided by structuring the situation by simply asking the child if he or she needs to go to the bathroom prior to entering the playroom.

Step 2: State the limit to the child (Level 1)

1. Be succinct and clear.

2. Phrase the limit in a forceful but pleasant tone. Change your voice from an acceptance level to one of authority.

3. In this order, catch the child's attention by saying the child's name, reflect his or her desire to do the prohibited action, then state the limit.

4. Next give the child an alternative structure (redirect) to allow the child to open up again and redirect his or her own play.

The following statement provides the limit and structure without restricting play too much. It allows the child to make a choice.

> Therapist: Kassim, remember I told you there are some things you cannot
> do in here. One thing you cannot do is spit on me. You are really
> mad. I bet you can make a mad face instead of spitting.

If the child persists in asking why, reflect his or her questions and then answer with a simple reason:

> Therapist: You want to know why you can't throw the ball at mirror. It might
> break. If the mirror breaks, it will be unsafe in here.

Step 3: Warning (Level 2)

If the child breaks the limit that you have just set (the second time this occurs in the session), remind the child of the first warning, reestablish the limit, and state what will happen if the limit is broken again. A warning is given so that the child knows beforehand what will happen if he or she breaks the limit and can decide whether to risk the consequences.

> Therapist: Kassim, remember what I just said about spitting. You are super
> angry at me. You can pretend to spit, but if you spit on me again,
> our time is up for today.

Step 4: Enforcement of consequences (Level 3)

Restate the rule and follow through with the consequences you warned the child about. Doing this is critical if you want the child to take you seriously. Use a firm but pleasant tone. You can stand up immediately or guide the child to the door to clearly convey your insistence that the child leave now because he or she has broken a limit (see guidelines for closing a session on page 58).

> Therapist: Kassim, you spit at me again, so now our time is up. You are
> really upset. I'll see you next time.

When limits are set this way, children will begin to learn that they are responsible for what happens to them. When children make a choice to break a limit after having been warned, they know what the results will be. After children learn that you mean what you say by your actions in following through, you will find that they do not tend to "limit out." Children do not want to lose time in the playroom.

For each subsequent session, start at the warning stage (Level 2) and progress to enforcement of consequences (Level 3) if necessary.

Your Turn: Should You Set the Limit?

In the following scenarios, determine whether you need to set a limit. Check "Yes" for limits you need to set and "No" for behaviors that do not require a limit. If you need to set a limit, provide a prosocial alternative for the child. You can check your answers against our responses and commentary on page 116.

1. Child wants to leave session early.   ☐ Yes   ☐ No

   Alternative: _____

   _____

2. Child wants to stand on the chair.   ☐ Yes   ☐ No

   Alternative: _____

   _____

3. Child spanks you.   ☐ Yes   ☐ No

   Alternative: _____

   _____

4. Child writes on your (or his own) face with marker.   ☐ Yes   ☐ No

   Alternative: _____

   _____

5. Child yells swear words.   ☐ Yes   ☐ No

   Alternative: _____

   _____

6. Child wants to take clothes off.   ☐ Yes   ☐ No

   Alternative: _____

   _____

7. Child plays with your hair.   ☐ Yes   ☐ No

   Alternative: _____

   _____

8. Child kisses you.   ☐ Yes   ☐ No

   Alternative:_____

   _____

9. Child wants to tie you up.   ☐ Yes   ☐ No

   Alternative:_____

   _____

10. Child brings in toys from home.   ☐ Yes   ☐ No

    Alternative:_____

    _____

11. Child wants to take home artwork.   ☐ Yes   ☐ No

    Alternative:_____

    _____

12. Child sucks on baby bottle.   ☐ Yes   ☐ No

    Alternative:_____

    _____

13. Child shoots at you with toy gun.   ☐ Yes   ☐ No

    Alternative:_____

    _____

14. Child says nasty things to you.   ☐ Yes   ☐ No

    Alternative:_____

    _____

15. Child exposes her private parts.   ☐ Yes   ☐ No

    Alternative:_____

    _____

Individual Therapist Limits

In addition to limits that maintain safety for the child, play therapist, and setting, you may also have limits that are individual to you. Here's an example: We like to have toy handcuffs in our playrooms. Children will use handcuffs in a number of ways: to restrain you, to attach themselves to something in the playroom (often symbolic for not wanting to leave), or even to connect themselves with you.

Sometimes a child will "arrest" you in session and want to handcuff your hands behind your back. Neither of us is bothered by this, but other play therapists do not feel comfortable with this type of restraint. If the therapist is not comfortable with the behavior, it will get in the way of rapport with the child. When this happens, it is necessary to give an acceptable alternative, such as handcuffing the play therapist's hands in front of the body. An appropriate limit could be "Aden, you really want me to feel powerless by handcuffing my hands behind my back. It makes you feel really strong and in control. I'm not comfortable with that, but you can handcuff my hands in front of my body."

We have found that children in play therapy are very understanding and accommodating to personal limits. Personal limits are not only acceptable but important in maintaining the therapeutic relationship. During a session, a play therapist is continually working on accepting the child (Ray, 2011). Providing the child with an alternative allows the child a way to play out what he or she needs and also allows the play therapist to remain accepting of the child.

June once supervised a play therapist who was in the last trimester of pregnancy, working with an especially active and impulsive six-year-old boy. She was in good physical condition and maintained her ability to be at the child's level, sitting on the floor. In session, the therapist did not seem herself; instead, she seemed distracted and worried, even though she had worked effectively with this boy during many high-intensity sessions. She was a very talented play therapist who did not easily get rattled, so something was getting in her way. During supervision, we addressed this issue. It turns out that while sitting on the floor in her advanced stage of pregnancy, she did not feel able to move and get around very quickly, something we often have to do during play therapy sessions. Upon further discussion, she revealed that she was worried about the safety of her unborn child. She was concerned that her active client might fall on her or impulsively throw something that she might not be able to dodge. She felt strongly about being on her client's level instead of sitting in the desk chair that was available in the room, and she did not want to limit the intensity of his play. We came up with a simple and very easy solution that made a huge difference in the playroom. Instead of sitting on the floor, she brought in a chair with short legs, lower to the floor. This made it easier for her to move, as opposed to getting up from a cross-legged position on the floor. She simply stated to her client, "Dan, I want you to be able to play the way you need to play, so I'm going to sit on this chair instead of how I usually sit right down on the floor." The boy was unfazed; the session went on with the usual intensity, but the play therapist was now better able to accept the child, feeling more in control of her own safety.

Closing the Play Therapy Session

Because children generally like the experience of play therapy and the play therapist, leaving the session can be a difficult transition. Stability is paramount in the play therapy relationship. Play therapists therefore need to close the session in a consistent way, easily identified by the child as the closing. Basically, you give two time warnings, then end the session:

- One time warning is given five minutes before the end of the playtime: "Josefina, there are five minutes of playtime left today."

- The last warning is given one minute before the end of session: "Josefina, we have one more minute left today."

- At the end of the session, say firmly but pleasantly: "Josefina, our time is up for today. We have to leave now."

    Tip: Use the child's name when giving time limits to get the child's attention and ground the child in the here and now.

If the child is reluctant to leave the room, reflect her feelings and restate that the session is ending. Using your body and voice to stress your message, do the following:

1. Stand straight up from your physical position at the child's level to your typical adult height.

2. If there is a light on, turn it off.

3. Go directly to the door and open it.

4. Change the tone of your voice from acceptance to a firm and clear intention.

5. Take the child gently by the back of the shoulder and guide the child in the direction of the door.

6. Explain to the child that for every extra minute, he or she will lose a minute from the next time.

7. After five minutes, explain that if the child she doesn't leave with you now, he or she cannot come next time.

    Tip: First reflect the child's feelings before attempting to enforce leaving.

No-Nos: Questions, Praise, and Self-Disclosure

In this section, we will address the use of questions, praise, and self-disclosure from several different perspectives. First, we will talk about why questions can cause problems in your communications with children in child-centered play therapy. This discussion covers the use of "taggers" and the role your level of confidence plays in turning fine listening responses like tracking and reflections into responses that are not favorable in child-centered play therapy (namely, questions). We will also talk about the questioning technique commonly referred to as the "whisper technique" (Kottman, 2010) and how this is relevant to role-playing.

No Questions

When we are training play therapists (and other mental health professionals, for that matter), we start with a rule that we hold our students and supervisees to without wavering. There are to be NO questions asked. The rationale behind this prohibition is that in order to learn to listen effectively, you need to eliminate questions from your clinical response repertoire.

Questions are typically asked from the perspective of the clinician. Axline (1969) reinforced that when the play therapist needs to know *why*, rapport is compromised. Therefore, questions are not appropriate from the child-centered perspective because they do not coincide with the Eight Basic Principles. Once the play therapist has asked a question, the child is no longer leading the session, and the play therapist is now the leader. Furthermore, questions tend to rush the process of therapy, which is also counter to the Eight Basic Principles. Patience is the key skill in NOT asking questions. If you are patient, you will find that most of your questions will get answered. We truly ask only two questions in child-centered play therapy: Do you need to go to the bathroom? and Do you need a tissue for that?

When you first start using reflections of feeling and tracking statements as responses, you may feel unnatural or robotic. Practice will help, and confidence in your reflective listening skills will come with that practice. Until you gain the confidence that comes with time, proper training, and supervision, you are likely to make tracking and reflective responses that sound like questions because of your inflection at the end of the statement. So a solid reflection like "You are really angry" will come out sounding like a question: "You are really angry?" Be patient with yourself and do what it takes to become more confident about your skills. This type of questioning will pass in time.

One more thing: Please promise us that you will never ask a child "How does that make you feel?" or "Why . . . ?" We do not want you to ask any questions in play therapy, but these two questions really make us want to scream. Here's why: First, you will not need to ask "How does that make you feel" because you will be observing the child and endeavoring to understand the child's phenomenological perspective so that you can reflect the feeling with accuracy. In the instances when you are inaccurate, some very cool things happen. Specifically, the child can correct you if you have created an atmosphere where the child feels safe and you can demonstrate that you can be wrong and still accept yourself. Second, children do not have a large affective vocabulary to draw from in order to answer questions (although their feelings vocabularies will increase as a consequence of routinely having their feelings reflected).

Next there are "why" questions. "Why" questions tend to put people, including children, on the defensive. In child-centered play therapy, you want children to feel safe and not as though they need to defend themselves. "Why" questions are also relatively unanswerable by children who have not yet reached particular milestones in cognitive development.

So don't ask questions because they will get in the way of listening and sticking to the Eight Basic Principles, and PLEASE do not ask the questions discussed in this section because, well, frankly, they are awful questions!

Your Turn: No Questions

Please change these commonly asked questions into listening responses. Sample answers can be found on page 120.

EXAMPLE:

And how does that make you feel?　　　*You are not sure how you are feeling.*

1. Why did you do that?　　　_____

_____

2. What could you have done differently?　_____

_____

3. How would you like to change this?　_____

_____

4. Why do you think that happened?   _____

_____

5. Do you want me to color with you?   _____

_____

Whisper technique

When you need clarification in role-plays, it is okay to use the "whisper technique" (Kottman, 2010) to obtain clarification from the child. For example, the child might say, "Okay, you be the dad." The therapist can reply in a whisper that demonstrates to the child that the play therapist is not yet taking on the role the child has assigned: "What kind of dad do you want me to be?" These questions can often be avoided by being patient and letting the role-play emerge. Another tip with regard to role-plays: Role-playing takes precedence over responding. If a child includes and directs you in a role-play, it is your job to follow that lead and stay in the role. More advanced and seasoned play therapists can often make listening responses while in role; however, until you have had additional training and supervision, stick to following the child's lead and directives.

What's a tagger, and why am I avoiding it?

A tagger is the little question we add to the end of a statement that changes a statement into a question. Here are two examples: "Leah, it's time for bed, *okay?*" and "You understand what we are saying about why you should not ask questions, *right?*" It is typical to use taggers in everyday speech. Listen to the people around you (yourself included), and you will be amazed at how frequently taggers are used. You need to be very careful about letting taggers sneak into your speech in play therapy because children are like little lawyers and will find the loopholes in your statements. Here's an example of a critical time when a tagger would get in the way: "Andrew, our session is over for today, *okay?*" Andrew could say "no," as if you were asking him for a response, which by including a tagger you actually just did. A potential power struggle could emerge, making the end of the session unpleasant for both you and Andrew and potentially jeopardizing your relationship.

It may be very difficult to rid yourself of these nasty taggers at first. There are several reasons they are so difficult to remove from your speech: First, they are ingrained. If you are part of a marginalized or devalued cultural group, you have been socialized to be unsure of yourself and will likely use taggers with relative consistency and frequency. Second, when you are feeling unsure or lack confidence, which we anticipate might be the case when you begin doing play therapy, you are likely to demonstrate your lack of confidence by including taggers in your speech. We would like you to work hard on eliminating taggers from your speech, *you know what we mean?*

No Praise

In many adult interactions with children, praise is a component. People use praise with children in the attempt to help build children's self-esteem. If you observe adults praising children, you will likely see many instances of empty or disingenuous praise. Because children are listening to verbal communications and are even more in tune with nonverbal communications, vocal tone, and inflections, they know when adults' praise is sincere or insincere. In child-centered play therapy, it's best to leave praise altogether out of your response repertoire.

You may be shocked to learn that praise is not an acceptable response to children in an approach where children are valued, honored, and respected. In fact, that is exactly why praise is not used. When praise is used as a response, the praiser is communicating his or her perspective. It is basically a judgment by the praiser. In child-centered play therapy, the focus is on the perspective of the child.

Here's an example to illustrate this point:

> Taylor: I did it. I made a basket.

> Praiser: I am so proud of you.

In this example, the child's esteem is connected to the adult's response. The child may initially feel good upon hearing the praise, but that positive feeling is based on what the praiser is communicating and not on the child's feelings of pride in the accomplishment. The praise and esteem are located outside of the child, so the child must rely on the outside source for validation and to feel good. The child does not own the positive perspective of self. When the source is external, the child needs that other person in order to feel good about himself or herself.

Observe the subtle, but critical differences in the example that follows:

> Taylor: I did it. I made a basket.

> Therapist: You are so proud and excited.

In this example, the therapist recognizes the child's perspective of self. The child owns the feelings of pride. The pride is located inside of the child, where it can be accessed at any time and not just when the child is in the presence of the praiser.

It is sometimes very difficult to leave praise outside of the play therapy relationship. However, if you follow the child-centered approach, you will need to do just that. Although praise is "nice," it is still a judgment. Child-centered play therapists do not stand in judgment of their clients.

In place of praise and judgments, we prefer to use esteem-building statements that do just that: build esteem within children. They help children to believe and trust in themselves and their abilities. These statements communicate that they are capable individuals and that they have opinions, preferences, and drives of their own. Look at the following exchange:

> Child: (Struggles with a puzzle, but keeps trying.) Look! I finished it!
>
> Adult: I'm so proud of you!

This is a very "nice" response. It is a response that communicates to the child that the adult is proud of what the child has done. Don't get us wrong: This is a perfectly acceptable response for a parent to make to a child! But it is not the *best* response to build esteem within the child and not an acceptable response in child-centered play therapy.

Let's look at another response:

> Child: (Struggles with a puzzle, but keeps trying.) Look! I finished it!
>
> Adult: *You* did it! It was hard, but *you* stuck with it until *you* got it!

This response is much richer. It shows the adult's excitement for what the child has done but puts the emphasis on the child's effort, ability, and achievement.

Your Turn: No Praise

This exercise includes examples of interactions with children that often elicit praise responses. Please correct the praise response with a response that demonstrates an understanding of the child's perspective, using either reflections of feeling or tracking responses. Refer to the preceding discussion for examples. Sample answers can be found on page 121.

1. Greg: I did it. Do you like it?

   Praiser: I am so proud of you. It's awesome.

   Therapist: _____

   _____

2. Jaielle: Here, catch.

   Praiser: That was a good throw.

   Therapist: _____

   _____

3. Eli: Look how tall I made the building.

   Praiser: Wow, you did a great job.

   Therapist: _____

   _____

4. Juanita: (Puts on princess crown.) I am the fairest in the land.

   Praiser: You look beautiful.

   Therapist: _____

   _____

5. Griffin: (Draws a picture, looks at the therapist, and smiles.)

   Praiser: That's a terrific picture.

   Therapist: _____

   _____

No Self-Disclosure

It does not make sense to use self-disclosure in child-centered play therapy sessions. If you are focusing on the child's perspective and phenomenological world, there is no reason for self-disclosure. In addition, children do not gain much from adult self-disclosures because children are egocentric. As much as children love us as their play therapists, they do not need us to change the agenda (and change the focus for ourselves through self-disclosure). Tiffany taught Jodi this concept. Tiffany had just had surgery and had missed a month of play therapy. Upon reengaging, Jodi said, "Welcome back. I bet having your tonsils out hurt." She said, "I feel better." Jodi responded, "I never had my tonsils out." Tiffany replied, "I don't care." Lesson learned: Self-disclosure is not consistent with the child-centered model.

Toys and Settings

On the following pages, you will find a recommended list of toys for the therapeutic playroom and some thoughts on various settings for the therapeutic playroom.

Toys for the Playroom

There are several general characteristics of toys chosen for the playroom. They should be sturdy and durable so that children can use them without being overly concerned about damaging them. It is important that the play therapy room be a consistent place, within the limits of practicality (Cochran et al., 2010). The same toys should be in the room each time, so you want toys that are inexpensive and easy to replace if they break or get damaged. Expensive toys or toys that hold special meaning for you do not belong in the playroom. The presence of these toys in the playroom will likely be distracting to you and may prevent you from sticking to the Eight Basic Principles. Furthermore, the toys in the playroom should allow for expression of feelings: Children in play therapy will express, regress, and aggress, and you want to supply toys so they can communicate all these experiences.

Ray (2001) encourages us to be thoughtful about each and every toy or play material in the playroom. She uses the following questions to assess which toys and play materials belong in the environment:

- What therapeutic purpose will this serve for children who use this room?

- How will this help children express themselves?

- How will this help me build a relationship with children?

Of course, YOU are the most important "toy" in the playroom, so don't get too caught up with having a perfect playroom with an extensive selection of toys. The toys listed here are the basics and will get you started. We have included a commentary to explain why toys listed are important in the playroom. We have also included some additional discussion regarding certain toys that are particularly useful. We learned about these toys from the most reliable sources—children!

Blocks

Children can build and create whatever they choose in the playroom. We recommend foam blocks because they stand up well and are less likely to injure you or the child if they come falling down or get thrown at you. They are expensive, but they are sturdy and even waterproof.

Mirror

Children like seeing what they look like. It is particularly fascinating to them as they try out the various aspects of their personality. Nonbreakable mirrors are available at a variety of retail stores.

Ball

A soft ball is your best bet here (see rationale regarding foam blocks). Children will often use a ball to bring you into the relationship through catch or other play that requires you to participate. A ball is a great tool for helping children communicate about relationships and competency.

Family/people puppets

The children Jodi works with rarely use puppets because Jodi just isn't a "puppet person." She'd like you to know this upfront so you can filter the following discussion about puppets through that knowledge. Many of our colleagues frequently use puppets, and there are two puppets in Jodi's playroom that she uses regularly (even with her negative puppet vibe). Both puppets are menacing: a dragon puppet and a crocodile puppet. It is important to have a varied collection. It is also important to have puppets whose mouths are not sewn shut. Children give voices to puppets (or vice versa), and when the mouth is sewn shut it is difficult for concrete thinkers to understand how communication can take place.

Dollhouse

Dollhouses are a great inclusion in the playroom. Essentially, the dollhouse allows the child to communicate about what happens or happened—or what they wish would happen or had happened at home. Dollhouse play is a way to visit a child's home from the child's phenomenological perspective. A dollhouse can be one of the more expensive items in the playroom. For this reason, you might check with friends or colleagues who have children to see if they have a used dollhouse that they would be willing to pass on. Consignment stores or garage sales are also good places to look for dollhouses.

Foam noodles

Foam noodles are inexpensive water toys, approximately five feet long and made of lightweight foam material. They come in a variety of colors. A very creative play therapist, Pam Gicale, taught us to cut these noodles in half, so now there are two foam cylinders to be used in lieu of swords or other weapons. This idea is brilliant, and here's why:

- It hurts a lot less when you get hit, poked, or otherwise struck with a noodle.

- Noodles are very inexpensive.

- They last and last, so they are a great investment.

- They are acceptable in playrooms where dedicated toy weapons would not be allowed.

Egg cartons (empty, of course)

Any empty box like a cereal box will also do. The purpose of including this item in the playroom is connected to limit setting. Often children will want to break or destroy something. They may feel enraged or just want to communicate to you what it is like to have something you value damaged beyond repair. Clearly, children cannot be permitted to break toys in the playroom. They can, however, be redirected through limit setting to items such as empty egg cartons or cereal boxes that they can destroy without the emotional consequences of feeling guilty, scared, or threatened. Having such items on hand allows you to remain centered in the Eight Basic Principles because you can both accept the child's feelings and keep the session grounded in reality.

Tea set

A tea set is another toy that allows relational themes to emerge. Play with the tea set is also a useful way for children to communicate about nurturance and connection. If you can't find a tea set, paper plates and cups will do.

Washable markers and paint

Art supplies allow for expression. We recommend washable markers or paint because they allow us to worry less about the ramifications of children's getting their clothes or bodies marked up. It is important to note that "washable" does not apply to every fabric or surface. In our experience, even washable markers or paint will leave a trace on skin.

Baby bottle

This is the perfect toy for children to express needs or desires to regress. Children appreciate being able to "be a baby" without the typical negative reaction they may get from adults and other children outside of the playroom. Keep your baby bottle filled with water. As with any toy that children put in their mouths, take care to sanitize.

Farm animals

Children can use farm animals in traditional ways. It also may be less threatening to demonstrate relational patterns using animals rather than people (Kottman, 2003). Therefore, having animal figures allows children the opportunity to communicate about people without having to do so directly.

Toy food

Many of the children we see clinically use the toy food in our playrooms during their sessions. Toy food seems to be among the most popular items, particularly when paired with the kitchen set (more about that to come). Toy food can be prepared, thrown around, eaten, fed to others, and even withheld. Children's interactions with food often show us how they are feeling in relationships with primary caregivers. We once shared a sibling set as clients who both routinely played out being denied food as punishment. As it turned out, these children were indeed being neglected in this way at home.

You can embrace cultural diversity by having a variety of plastic food replicas, including ethnic food choices. Some foods, particularly ethnically diverse foods, are difficult to find in plastic toy form. You can still incorporate these food selections by using empty (and thoroughly cleaned) boxes or containers. Empty spice containers are a nice addition because even after they have been cleaned, the scent of the spice remains. It is the scent of the spice that some children will be drawn to, comforted by, or curious about. Essentially, the scent adds another element to the experience, drawing on powerful connections to the olfactory experience.

Last, food containers in the playroom also allow for easy redirection in limit setting. When a child needs to be offered choices about what he or she can destroy, used cereal boxes and spice containers do the trick.

Kitchen set

A brand new kitchen set for your playroom is likely to be expensive. We encourage you to ask around and check your resources to see if you can find a gently used one. The reason we suggest a gently used one is that you will be less likely to be distracted by the constant wear and tear on this item. If you have the space and means, a kitchen set is a true asset to your therapeutic playroom.

The kitchen is the hub of the action and interaction in the playroom, just as it is in many homes. Having the kitchen set in the playroom makes it easier for children to act out their perspectives of family and home life. Remember, children play out their lives in play and play therapy, so children will show and communicate a great deal through their play with this familiar prop. Common themes of nurturance, relationships, power, and control are frequently played out with this toy.

Telephone (two)

Telephones are wonderful metaphors for communication. In the playroom, we like to have two, so if the child wants to include us in the play, it is easily done. When children use the phone in the playroom, we are alert to whom they are calling, talking to, and cannot get connected with, and certainly to how they are responding verbally and nonverbally.

Play-Doh or clay

Play-Doh or modeling clay is a nice addition to a playroom. Children can use this medium to create almost anything. The tactile experience alone can be very powerful for some children. If you have carpeted floors, be thoughtful about how you limit the use of these materials. It is also reasonable to limit mixing Play-Doh and clay with water, sand, or paints so that the material will not need to be replaced as often. Some of you may not be able to handle the thought of having your Play-Doh colors mixed together. If this is the case, you may want to have two separate containers, one for material that cannot be mixed with other colors and one for material that can. Your idiosyncratic beliefs and behaviors will affect your adherence to the Eight Basic Principles. Therefore, it behooves you to be thoughtful about the process so that you can be comfortable, permissive, and therapeutic.

Toy soldiers

Small figures like army men are useful because they are easy to manipulate and can help children communicate about group dynamics, fear, protection, and safety. (By the way, where are the army women?)

Doctor's kit

Baby doll

It's important to have a baby doll (even better to have two) in your therapeutic playroom. Through play with dolls, children are able to communicate vast amounts of information about their perspectives, including but not limited to themselves, their families, and their view of younger children, nurturance, and caretaking/caregiving. Play therapists can honor diversity by having baby dolls that are representative of the multicultural society in which we live.

Camera

A toy camera is sometimes difficult to find because many of them have images already programmed on them, and what the child sees through the lens has already been decided. We prefer real cameras without batteries or film. These are easy to find and inexpensive, and the 35mm models are available for just a few dollars at a garage sale or thrift store. Cameras allow children to demonstrate what they want to remember. They are also fine vehicles for communicating important themes in play therapy like memory, regression, relationships, and resilience.

Paper

We keep paper in the playroom as a means for children to create what they want or need. We do limit the paper to three pieces because we have had experiences in which there has been a large stack of paper and a child has scribbled on every page. That might not be a big deal to you, but if you find it irritating, you may not able to adhere to the Eight Basic Principles.

Dinosaurs

Dinosaurs can be menacing and are therefore useful for the child to communicate fear or anger. They can also be used by children in the playroom to communicate about relationships (refer to the preceding discussion regarding farm animals).

Bop bag

Some professionals do not believe that a bop bag is an appropriate toy to have in the playroom. The rationale for this argument is that the bop bag serves to increase aggression. Our experience has been the contrary. It's true that many children use the bop bag to demonstrate aggression, but it is also regularly used to protect, defend, or befriend. Finding a bop bag that is durable enough to withstand several aggressive children per week is a challenge. Some definitely hold up better with regular and frequent use, and we would recommend seeking them out.

When children are interacting with toys (or you and toys), it is important that you do not label specific toys. To gain an understanding of the child's perspective, child-centered play therapists wait for the child to designate what a particular toy is. For instance, a child could use a hat as a bowl or a stethoscope as a utility belt. If the play therapist says something like "You found a hat," it could detract from the child's creativity and simultaneously shift the focus from the child's to the therapist's perception. It is common to slip up in the playroom and name toys. We want you to recognize that refraining from doing so will take some practice.

Along with labeling toys, it is not appropriate to correct the child in child-centered play therapy. For example, you would not correct the child if he labeled a toy hammer a screwdriver. Most of our interactions as adults with children involve correction. The lack of correction is another aspect of the child-centered play therapy relationship that sets it apart from other adult-child relationships. Children are not scrutinized in this relationship for making mistakes or not knowing the proper names of certain items. The correcting dynamic frequently comes up in relation to toys; however, the goal of not correcting children in play therapy extends beyond this scenario.

Settings for the Playroom

This section focuses on creating the physical environment for play therapy sessions. This is probably a good time to remind you that the physical setting, including what toys you have available, is far less important than the relationship you have with the child. The relationship is what matters most. Even if you have a small, dark play therapy room, with only a few of the most basic toys, play therapy can happen because of you and what you bring as the play therapist.

In an ideal world, we have the space to create a play therapy room that meets many of the suggested specifics in terms of amount of space, flooring, equipment, lighting, and toys. Ray (2001) suggests that the playroom allow enough space for a child to move freely without becoming overwhelmed with too much space. Landreth (2002) suggests that an ideal playroom be 12 by 15 feet.

A room totally devoted to play therapy is a luxury in many schools and agencies. More often than not, the space we have for conducting play therapy sessions is not ideal. Some of the challenges we have faced in creating a space are very small rooms, having to share space with other play therapists, sharing the room with other non–play therapists, and needing to use the play therapy room also as an office. We have even needed to create a portable play therapy room, when traveling to several different schools and doing home-based work.

We were lucky enough to get a room that was a dedicated play therapy space in an elementary school. The unique thing about this room was that it was actually a closet. It was in the basement of the school, dark, damp and cold—not exactly the environment that conveyed positivity or hope. The first thing we needed to do to make this room work was change our attitude about the space. Rather than be disappointed, we changed our mindset and focused instead on appreciating having been given the opportunity and the knowledge that the power of play therapy is not limited by the physical environment. We brought in bright lighting, made thoughtful decisions about what toys to include and which we could live without (no full-size dollhouse in that room; a small one would do), and decorated the room with colorful, engaging artwork.

The most important lesson we learned in that space was that the relationship is truly the key to play therapy. It did not matter to a single child that there were no windows, that our personal space was somewhat compromised, or that the room smelled a bit dank. What mattered was that, each week, there was time in their day when someone would invite them into this very special room, where they felt accepted, important, and understood. It is the structure and consistency of the play therapy room and the play therapist that gives many children a sense of predictability and security that they may not have anywhere else in their world.

Shared space is also a challenge, whether it is with other play therapists or other practitioners. When you share a room with other play therapists, communication is the key. Collaborating on what toys to include in the room and what toys not to include is important. It can throw off both child and play therapist to come into the play therapy room and be surprised by new toys. We don't include board games in our therapeutic playrooms because we feel it gets in the way of the child's creativity and, frequently, the play becomes more about the structure and rules of the game than the child. Therefore, when sharing a play therapy room with a colleague, we would have to come to some agreement about the inclusion of board games in the room.

Taking care of the room and the toys in it is also paramount in sharing space successfully. Again, communication about expectations is key. What happens if a toy breaks during a session you are conducting? What if the caps were left off all the markers, and now they are dried out? You will want to consider these issues, even if they seem rather insignificant, because you need to maintain your focus on the child during the play therapy session, not on what to do because your colleague used up all the paper and now you have none available for your session.

A foundation of communication is imperative whether you are sharing a your space with another play therapist or with a colleague who does not use a play therapy approach. An additional concern arises when the colleague you share space with is not a play therapist. It will behoove you to have some storage space for your toys so that the office can look like an office and not a playroom. This is also the case when you don't have to share space with someone else but when your playroom has to double as a more traditional counseling office.

Finally, when you are a traveling play therapist, you need to compromise, just as play therapists who have smaller offices do. You'll want to assess which of your toys get the most action and bring those. Luckily, many storage options can give you the ability to have a decent toy choice without being prohibitive in terms of portability. In a pinch, a large suitcase will work—even better if it has wheels. You may not be able to get all the suggested toys and materials. Having a few key items is really all you need to get started: a baby doll and baby bottles; clay, paints, paper, and crayons; a toy gun and toy soldiers; a toy car; puppets; and a telephone.

Regardless of the physical set-up of your play therapy space, it is important to keep in mind is that consistency is the key. Children feel more safe and settled if they can count on the playroom or play space and the toys in it to be basically the same each session. Giving children a sense of safety and stability is fundamental to their healing and growth.

PART 4

Ready for Practice (and Play)

If you have made it to this point of the book, you are probably feeling ready to dive into the world of play therapy. We can remember feeling that way, too. Now that you have an overall idea of what play therapy takes—a good understanding of the philosophy, skills needed, and character required—it's time to set the stage for play therapy to happen.

This section contains discussion and exercises to ready you for the practice of play therapy. We want to again remind you that this workbook is not a substitute for training and supervision. This workbook is designed to augment training and supervision by reinforcing skills and providing multiple ways of learning the philosophy and the approach. In this section, we will discuss the structure of the play therapy session and themes and "firsts" that occur in child-centered therapy, also addressing concerns beginning play therapists have about termination issues and the progression of a child's play. We will also share with you the questions our students and supervisees typically ask as they prepare for their very first play therapy session.

It is difficult to judge your effectiveness in the early stages of your development as a play therapist. You will complete an exercise designed to help you assess the impact of the responses you are making in play therapy. We have also included a comprehensive list of treatment plan goals that are consistent with the child-centered approach. The impetus for the creation and inclusion of this information comes directly from the mental health field. Many of our supervisees struggle with having to fit the child-centered approach into agency-based paperwork and documentation designed specifically for other approaches to counseling children. We hope you find this a useful inclusion.

Last, you will find a unique overview of the benefits of child-centered play therapy, described from an adult-imagined perspective of the child. This is included to help center you as you embark on the magical relationship that is achieved through the child-centered play therapy approach.

Structuring the Play Therapy Session: The Cookbook Version

This page is included to ground you in the overall structure needed to conduct a play therapy session.

Opening

[Name] _____ , this is very special room. You can do almost anything in here. If there is something you can't do, I will tell you. You can also say anything.

Tip: You do not need to say this every session. We typically say it for the first three to five sessions. With children who have developmental delays, we may say it a few more times. If a child has been away from play therapy for an extended time, we will say it again as a reminder the first time back into the playroom.

Limit Setting

Level 1

[Name] _____ , remember I told you there are some things you cannot do in here. One thing you cannot do is _____.

- Reflect.

- Redirect.

    EXAMPLE: <u>Kristie,</u> remember I told you there are some things you cannot do in here. One thing you cannot do is <u>put paint on my face.</u> You really want me to know how messy that feels. You can put paint on my hands or on the doll.

Level 2

[Name] _____ , remember before I told you that you could not _____. If you _____ again, our session will be over for today.

- Reflect.

- Redirect.

    EXAMPLE: <u>Kristie,</u> remember before I told you that you could not <u>put paint on my face.</u> If you <u>put paint on my face</u> again, our session will be over for today. You're mad that I will not let you put the wet, sticky paint on my face. You can make my hands as yucky as you want.

Level 3

[Name] _____ , our session is over for today.

- Reflect.

- Repeat (if necessary).

  EXAMPLES:

  Kristie, our session is over for today. You hate that you have to go.

  Stacey, our session is over for today. I will see you next time.

Time

[Name] _____ , you have *five minutes* left today.

- Reflect.

[Name] _____ , you have *one minute* left today.

- Reflect.

Closing

[Name] _____ , our session is over for today. I'll see you next time.

- Reflect.

Themes

Throughout the child's experience in play therapy, the play therapist will begin to notice that certain actions, patterns, and communications are more prevalent than others. These recurring patterns are referred to as *themes* in the play therapy process, and they happen over and over again in sessions or over time. Themes are a valuable tool in assessing what is important to the child from the child's perspective. They allow you a peek inside the child's phenomenological world so that you can get a feel for what that child is experiencing.

Although sometimes themes are very obvious, at other times they are more subtle. The detection of themes may vary depending on the observer, making them somewhat subjective. (In other words, two play therapists may view the same session in two different ways.) We often tell our supervisees that it is one thing to *view* a session, but it is another thing entirely to be *in* a session, so what we're seeing or feeling as we observe it may differ from their experience in the playroom.

Themes also help in conceptualizing the case because they capture the "big picture" and give insight into what is going on in the child's life outside the playroom. For example, if a child frequently plays out a need for power and control in the playroom and over the play therapist, it could be an indication that the child feels powerless in the world outside the playroom. Another example would be a child who often exhibits behaviors consistent with regression, such as sucking on a baby bottle, whining, or needing to have things done for her that she is able to do for herself. When children are stressed in their lives, they often regress, so this behavior may speak to the child's needing the safety and security of going back to a more comfortable time in her life. Themes may change frequently, and many themes may occur within one session.

Themes are a valuable consultation tool in that they allow the play therapist to talk about the child's play therapy process, yet still respect confidentiality (Mullen & Rickli, 2011). For instance, if a child client consistently plays out that he wants to be taken care of, this is something that may be communicated to the parent or caregiver. The theme of nurturance can help the therapist address the child's need outside the session. Without giving away that the child sucked on the baby bottle or that the child was showing more dependence than usual, the therapist might say, "I notice some nurturance play in Courtney's recent sessions. Sometimes this means that a child could use some extra one-on-one time. Do you think you can set aside 10 minutes before the day starts to have a little extra cuddle time with her?" Obviously, this would apply if the therapist felt that the child's nurturing play demonstrated a need.

Other times, children may show a nurturing theme by checking themselves and the play therapist out with the doctor's kit and stethoscope. They may be demonstrating with this type of nurturance play that they are able to care for themselves and even have enough confidence that they are able to care for the play therapist. You will know, with experience, what children are demonstrating.

A change in themes can also help the play therapist measure progress in the play-room. If a child who previously exhibited regressive play begins to demonstrate less dependency on the play therapist and has not shown the same regressive type of play, that may indicate that the child has moved on in the process toward growth and healing.

Sometimes a child may suddenly show a theme of confusion and chaos in his play, and this change is something a play therapist should be alert to. In this case, you might say, "I notice that Cole's play is showing some signs of confusion. Have there been some changes going on in his life that might help me to understand him better?" Believe it or not, many caregivers will fail to tell you of major changes going on in the child's life, usually because they don't understand the connection between the child's behavior and what is taking place in the home. They often do not think the child is aware of what is happening, even saying things like "We haven't told him yet that we're separating." Because children are incredible readers of nonverbal behavior, they are able to sense and feel what is going on in the home without being formally told.

Children will demonstrate their perspective of the world in their play. Children may use different toys or behaviors to demonstrate the saliency of their issues. Play therapists are alert to recurring themes in children's play within each session and throughout treatment. Common themes in children's play include the following.

Anger

Themes of anger emerge in many kinds of play. Often children will demonstrate this theme in role-plays, in which they illuminate the dynamics between characters.

Power/control

This theme emerges at some point in every child's play because children in our dominant adult culture are afforded few opportunities for either power or control. This theme is often obvious in the child's relationship with the play therapist.

Grief/loss

Children (like adults) experience tangible and intangible death and nondeath losses (Fiorini & Mullen, 2006). Themes of loss are therefore incredibly common in children's play. Children share the theme of grief and loss around losses as divergent as losing a tooth, moving, death, and military deployment of a parent.

Trust/betrayal/boundaries

Children referred for therapy are often responding to circumstances of trust and betrayal. Play therapists can anticipate seeing this theme in the play of many children. It is likely to emerge even in the first session if the child is unsure about trusting the play therapist.

Fear

The world can be a very scary place for children. The culture of adulthood does a fine job of creating and supporting childhood fears. (When Jodi's own children indicate being afraid of monsters, she usually says something that illuminates this perspective: "Monsters are things grown-ups make up to scare children.") Children will show you their fears and also want you to be afraid.

Protection/safety/boundaries

Protection, safety, and boundaries are preeminent for many children who find their way into the therapeutic playroom. This theme is frequently demonstrated as children experiment with what it would be like to be safe and/or protected.

Self-esteem

Some children demonstrate through their play how they feel about themselves. These children often share the perspective of self-esteem through competency play.

Attention

Children need attention because it is how they gain significance (Kottman, 2003). Because many children's needs for attention go unmet, you can expect that they will crop up in the playroom. Verbal cues for this theme are evident when the child says "look" or "watch."

Overwhelmed/chaos

Children can get stressed out and overwhelmed. Many children are in circumstances where they have no stability and the adults in their life offer little consistency. These children are likely to be overwhelmed and demonstrate their distress in the playroom.

Their play is chaotic, or they create an overwhelming mess to give the play therapist a sense of their experience.

Loyalty

It's difficult for children to grapple with issues of loyalty. This theme often is present in the play of children in the foster care system and in children who are in the middle of custody disputes. In their sessions, they play out the simultaneous pushes and pulls they experience.

Confusion

The world and relationships are particularly confusing to children. So many mixed messages are sent to children that they are likely to try to work out some of their confusion in play therapy sessions. Here's an example: Jodi's client Jonathon, eight years old, entered the playroom and said, "I don't get it. How come I can't hit my brother?" Jodi reflected, "It's confusing to you why that would not be okay." Jonathon replied, "No, that's not it. Why can't I hit my brother, but my mom can hit me?"

Nurturance

Regression, caretaking, and medical play can be characteristic of the play of children expressing the theme of nurturance.

Perfection

Children who express the theme of perfection in their sessions appear internally "uptight." In the playroom, they sometimes get annoyed when things are not exactly as they were in the previous session.

Guilt

Themes of guilt emerge from children's play in play therapy. To determine whether guilt is the theme, we listen for key words like *sorry* or play that demonstrates feeling bad after the consequences of an action are manifested.

This list of themes is not all inclusive—sometimes it helps to discern a theme if you can think of a "title" for a session or series of sessions. To repeat: Teasing out the themes helps with case conceptualization and allows you to talk respectfully and knowledgably about the child without disclosing specifics with other stakeholders in the child's life.

Your Turn: Name That Theme

As already stated, themes in play therapy can be rather subjective, meaning that two play therapists may view the same session differently in terms of theme. For the following behaviors, try to come up with at least one theme that a child might be demonstrating. We've included some that are more "cut and dried" than others. Obviously, as we've stated throughout this workbook, without actually being with a child in a session, you are somewhat at a disadvantage trying to ascertain what themes may be present, but we hope you'll give it a try. As extra practice, we would like you to think of a response statement, either a reflection of feeling or a tracking statement. The answers provided on page 121 are suggestions and are not indicative of the only correct answers.

1. Child repeatedly says to the play therapist, "Watch this!" or "Look!"

   Theme(s): _____

   Response: _____

2. Child uses items from the doctor kit and examines herself with the stethoscope.

   Theme(s): _____

   Response: _____

3. Child's dollhouse play consistently shows people or things falling off surfaces and in other precarious situations.

   Theme(s): _____

   Response: _____

4. Child punches and kicks the bop bag.

   Theme(s): _____

   Response: _____

5. Child enters the playroom and wanders around calmly, checking out various items.

   Theme(s): _____

   Response: _____

6. Child alternates between attempting to do things for himself and asking for help.

   Theme(s): _____

   Response: _____

7. Child organizes the playroom.

   Theme(s): _____

   Response: _____

8. Child attempts to draw a picture but throws it away and starts again and again.

   Theme(s): _____

   Response: _____

9. Child repeatedly tells the play therapist what to do and how to do it.

   Theme(s): _____

   Response: _____

10. Child attempts to undress the play therapist or self.

    Theme(s): _____

    Response: _____

Firsts

Children move at their own pace in child-centered play therapy. Adults often perceive the pace of children to be painfully slow. However, play therapists are aware of "firsts" evident in the play therapy session. Firsts are demonstrations of growth and change and are often prosocial in nature. It behooves play therapists (and their child client) to share firsts with other supportive adults in the child's life, like parents and teachers. The following is a list of common firsts or signs of growth.

In session, the child _____ for the first time.

- Uses the play therapist's name

- Demonstrates manners (e.g., says "please," "thank you," "excuse me")

- Asks for help or doesn't ask for help

- Leaves the room at the end of session without incident

- Limits his or her own behavior

- Makes eye contact

- Smiles, laughs, hums

- Verbalizes

- Uses feelings words

- Uses words that the therapist has used previously

- Includes the play therapist in his or her play

Because these firsts are often prosocial and most certainly a sign of growth, healing, and change, we not only look for and share the firsts that we see in children during their play therapy sessions, we also ask about firsts in other settings. For example, we ask parents about what new things they are seeing at home: "Have there been any surprises?" "What new things has your child done?" We find this technique also works with educators and other professionals who deal with the child. We might ask the classroom teacher, "What is one thing different that you have noticed in this child over the last month?"

You may observe that we structure these questions in a way that suggests change and firsts are happening. This is purposeful. We want to help other adults focus on growth rather than what is still frustrating about the child. In some ways, we are asking them to be part of a team of "first" detectives. Questions asked this way direct parents and other adults to focus on what's changing, growing, and healing, even if the process is slow and imperfect.

The other day, one of us received a text from a parent after her child's play therapy session. This is a child with significant mental health needs. The text said, "I don't know what happened in that session or in the past few weeks, but I have to tell you I am thrilled. Today for the first time in MONTHS my child sat down and did her homework!!! No fit, no tears, no throwing things, no screaming. THANK YOU." As you can see from this example, firsts are powerful; seeing and experiencing that first gave this parent hope and likely changed the whole feeling in that family's home that night.

Stages of Child-Centered Play Therapy

In general, children involved in child-centered play therapy will progress through stages. Knowledge of these stages is valuable in assessing the child's growth and change. Although child-centered play therapy is child directed, and each child's process is unique, there are still some commonalities. Stages help the play therapist track therapeutic progress both inside and outside of the therapeutic playroom (Cochran, 2010). There is no prescribed length of time for any of these stages because children move at their own pace.

Stage 1: Warm-up

This stage of therapy is characterized by the forming of the relationship and starts from the first second you come in contact with the child. The child may ask a considerable number of questions during this time. The child may also test you. Keep in mind that play therapy is an experience like no other and that the play therapist is a person like no other to children. Usually, an adult decides things for children and tells them what to do, so the self-direction and freedom is often hard for children to believe at the beginning: "Can I really do just about anything in here?" "Can I really say anything?" This warm-up stage may last up to two months. It will be longer for children with attachment difficulties or histories characterized by loss, abandonment, or betrayal.

Stage 2: Aggression and Pain

At this point, children will understand how things work with regard to the therapeutic relationship. They will have developed the trust in the relationship that tells them that the play therapist really does accept them unconditionally. They understand how limits work and that they have choices. With all of that behind them, they are now free to move forward, knowing that the environment is a safe one to work on their issues. Children will demonstrate their anger and pain during this stage, and it can be intense. Their perceptions may not match the reality of what has actually happened. However, children's perceptions will match their affective reality. Their perception of what has happened to them will impact their feelings about events.

Stage 3: Dependence and Independence

By this stage, a child has shown some negative aspects of self to the play therapist through the aggression, anger, and controlling play of Stage 2. At this stage, a child can allow vulnerability to show in the form of dependence, loss, grief, and sadness.

The child in this stage will want you to do or not do for him. A child may play out a need for nurturance, or he may feel the need to take care of others. Children will test their independence and dependence. They may show regression in the playroom and ask you to help them with tasks they've already mastered.

Stage 4: Mastery

At the mastery stage of therapy, there will be a change in play (see the following discussion of termination). Children will consistently demonstrate competency in this stage. Their play will be playful. (With experience, you will be able to see and feel the difference between playful play and working play.) Children will demonstrate socially appropriate behaviors in and out of the play therapy sessions.

Stage 5: Relationship Building

At this stage, the child may return to testing the relationship. She may show fear and confusion about the pending termination of the relationship. The child needs to know that even though you will no longer be seeing her in therapy, the relationship is an important one.

Is the Child Ready for Termination?

Determining when it is time for termination in child-centered play therapy is a difficult task. An accurate determination assumes that the therapist has paid close attention to themes and firsts. A child who is ready for termination no longer will display themes that were evident previously in therapy, and the child will consistently demonstrate prosocial firsts. The child may seem bored, may leave the session before the time has run out, and even say, "I don't want to come see you anymore."

Ideally, child-centered play therapy is child-centered to the end. Some changes in the child to consider are as follows:

The child . . .

- Is less dependent.

- Is less confused.

- Expresses needs openly.

- Is able to focus on self.

- Accepts responsibility for own actions and feelings.

- Limits own behavior appropriately.

- Is more inner directed.

- Is less rigid.

- Is consistently demonstrating prosocial behavior outside of sessions.

- Is more tolerant of the unpredictability of life.

- Initiates activities with assurance and confidence.

- Is cooperative but not conforming.

- Expresses anger appropriately and prosocially.

- Is consistently in a relatively good mood.

- Is more accepting of self, even after making mistakes.

- Is able to play out story sequences; the play has direction and makes sense.

- Shows play that has lightheartedness about it; the play is playful.

One thing that we have noticed in our years of doing this work is that pending discharge from play therapy services affects the child, caregivers, and even the play therapist. It is intuitive to recognize that the child will be impacted by termination from play therapy services. It is somewhat more surprising that caregivers and the play therapist also will be impacted. A little planning is helpful in this situation, letting the child and family know they are healthy and ready. We like using a countdown, showing children on a calendar. We make sure, of course, that we remain thoughtful and responsive to the child's perspective of saying good-bye.

Even beginning play therapists notice that children LOVE coming to play therapy. The one-to-one attention, feeling listened to and understood, and being respected make the play therapy relationship and the experience in play therapy sessions powerful and magical. Children appreciate this. What happens on occasion is that even though a child no longer needs services, the child still wants to come to play therapy. Jodi worked with an eight-year-old boy who was clearly ready for discharge. He was healthy and happy, and his relationships were good. Jodi shared with him that soon it would be time to say good-bye and asked, "How many more times would you like to come see me—one, two, or three?" His response was "I want to come until I am 16!" The boy's dad felt similarly. He said, "I know he's in a really good way and has been for months, but what if the anxiety and depression return?" This dad, like a lot of other parents and caregivers, are reluctant to support termination. They are scared. It takes a lot for parents to trust you with their child and to admit they need help (Mullen & Rickli, 2011). Reluctance on the part of parents at termination usually requires some additional parent consultation with a focus on strengths so that discharge from services does not produce unnecessary anxiety in the family.

Frequently, play therapy interventions—whether in agency-based, school, or private practice settings—do not end in an ideal way. Rather than ending when the process is complete, they end because of other variables that do not fall under the control of the child, parent, or play therapist. Many of the children we have worked with could be considered transient. The families of these kids move frequently and without much advance planning. Some of the children we work with have a change in custody or other circumstances that preclude us from seeing the play therapy process all the way through. This kind of termination is typically difficult for the play therapist (Landreth, 2002).

Because children rarely make decisions about their play therapy treatment, you can expect that will also be true when it comes to termination from play therapy services. We have noticed that play therapy services are frequently cut short because of the life circumstances of the family or because the family is not seeing results fast enough or of the type they wanted. We once had a four-year-old child who was removed from play therapy services by a family court judge who cited play therapy as empowering the child. Yes, you read that correctly: The judge indicated that empowering the child was a problem.

Our suggestion for dealing with terminations that are out of your control is to get good supervision. It is normal to feel angry and even sad when a child who was responding well to services is removed from your care. However, if that anger and sadness is not processed, it will fester and affect your work and professionalism. Take care of yourself by getting quality supervision from a more seasoned professional play therapist.

Commonly Asked Questions About Child-Centered Play Therapy

As instructors and supervisors of child-centered play therapy, we have observed that some questions are typical among professionals developing their play therapy craft. We have included some of the most common ones we have been asked by students, supervisees, and even parents. Your ability to answer these questions is a good way to assess what you have learned and what you still need help with, as well as your confidence level.

Your Turn: Commonly Asked Questions

Here are some situations that may occur in play therapy. Please attempt to answer each question. Answers and discussion can be found on page 124.

1. What if the child will not talk?

2. What if the child wants to bring in a friend, parent, sibling?

3. What about sand, paint, water, MESSES?

4. What do you do when the child won't leave the playroom?

5. What about swearing, cussing, or hate language?

6. What about having toy guns in the playroom?

7. What if the child wants to leave the session early?

8. What about settings where noise in the playroom is a factor to others in close proximity?

9. What if the child is being rude to the play therapist?

10. What if the child tells others he or she can use bad words in session?

11. What if a child puts toys in his or her mouth?

12. What if a child breaks toys?

13. What if a child wants to bring in a toy from home?

14. What about interruptions from others during play therapy sessions?

15. What if a child discloses abuse during a session?

16. What if a child doesn't feel well and does not want to play or participate?

17. How can play therapists honor diversity?

18. What do you do when a child tells you he or she loves you?

19. What should you do if the child falls asleep in session?

Evaluating the Impact of the Play Therapist's Responses

The play therapist should be able to assess the ongoing impact of his or her responses on the child. It is the play therapist's responsibility to ascertain when responses are accurate, inaccurate, therapeutic, nontherapeutic, tolerable, and/or threatening to the child.

Your Turn: Evaluating Therapist Responses

What do the following actions suggest about the play therapist's responses to the child? Check all that apply. Answers and discussion can be found on page 127.

Behavior	Accurate	Inaccurate	Therapeutic	Non-therapeutic	Tolerable	Threatening
1. Child moves closer to play therapist.	☐	☐	☐	☐	☐	☐
2. Child moves away from play therapist.	☐	☐	☐	☐	☐	☐
3. Play intensifies.	☐	☐	☐	☐	☐	☐
4. Child uses play therapist's words.	☐	☐	☐	☐	☐	☐
5. Child corrects play therapist.	☐	☐	☐	☐	☐	☐
6. Child turns away from play therapist.	☐	☐	☐	☐	☐	☐
7. Child invites play therapist into play.	☐	☐	☐	☐	☐	☐
8. Child tells play therapist to shut up, stop talking.	☐	☐	☐	☐	☐	☐
9. Child nods "yes" after response.	☐	☐	☐	☐	☐	☐
10. Child wants to end session.	☐	☐	☐	☐	☐	☐
11. Child's play changes abruptly.	☐	☐	☐	☐	☐	☐
12. Child's play is additive.	☐	☐	☐	☐	☐	☐
13. Child smiles.	☐	☐	☐	☐	☐	☐
14. Child looks at the play therapist.	☐	☐	☐	☐	☐	☐
15. Child ignores the play therapist.	☐	☐	☐	☐	☐	☐

Treatment Goals Consistent with Child-Centered Play Therapy

Many clinicians who use a play therapy approach as part of their clinical work are concerned about how to include play therapy in formal treatment plans and in requests for treatment from third-party payers. We have translated the language of the play therapy approach here so that is suitable for treatment plans. We have found that the way the goals of play therapy are stated below also can be very useful in communication with other professionals as well as in consultation with parents (see Mullen & Rickli, 2011, for a more in-depth discussion of consultation).

Family Problems

- Child will demonstrate improved communication skills with parents.

- Child will demonstrate improved communication skills with siblings.

- Child will demonstrate improved communication skills with extended family members.

- Child will demonstrate improved relational skills with parents.

- Child will demonstrate improved relational skills with siblings.

- Child will demonstrate improved relational skills with extended family members.

- Child will be able to communicate feelings in a developmentally appropriate fashion.

- Child will respect boundaries and limits set by family members within normal limits for age and developmental ability.

- Child will demonstrate prosocial skills.

- Child will demonstrate problem-solving skills.

Educational Problems

- Child will demonstrate improved communication skills with teachers and educational staff.

- Child will demonstrate improved communication skills with peers.

- Child will demonstrate improved relational skills with teachers and educational staff.

- Child will demonstrate improved relational skills with peers.

- Child will respect boundaries and limits set by teachers and educational staff within normal limits for age and developmental ability.

- Child will respect boundaries and limits set by peers within normal limits for age and developmental ability.

- Child will use time in play therapy to demonstrate aggression, regression, and expression that is not appropriate for the classroom.

- Child will demonstrate prosocial skills.

- Child will demonstrate problem-solving skills.

- Child will express emotional containment in the classroom.

- Child will seek appropriate support services in the school.

Mental Health Problems

- Child will engage in the play therapy process.

- Child will respect boundaries and limits set by the play therapist.

- Child will begin to express feelings verbally.

- Child's acting out behavior (anger, depression, anxiety) will abate.

- Child will be able to demonstrate insight.

- Child will be able to set culturally appropriate boundaries.

- Child will use play therapy sessions to explore mental health issues.

- Child's mood will stabilize.

- Child will share his or her perspective of the experience of trauma.

- Child will make prosocial choices.

- Child will demonstrate emotional problem solving.

- Child will smile and laugh at appropriate times.

- Child's mood and affect will be congruent.

- Child will express a complex variety of feelings.

- Permission to be different.

- Permission to discover, appreciate, and develop your inner self.

- Permission to make mistakes.

- Permission to learn from your mistakes.

- Permission to move at your own pace.

- Permission to direct your own behavior.

- Permission to make choices.

- Permission to self-discipline.

- Permission to self-correct.

- Permission to experience negative emotions.

- Permission to feel.

- Permission to have a warm, trusting relationship with an adult.

- Permission to tell your story in their own way.

- Permission to love.

- Permission to test out who you want to be.

- Permission to make things up.

- Permission to achieve success.

- Permission to manage your emotions.

- Permission to be cooperative.

- Permission to say no.

- Permission to resist authority.

- Permission to be a child.

- Permission to be quiet.

- Permission to cry.

- Permission to be a baby.

- Permission to feel sorry for yourself.

- Permission to think.

- Permission to show anger.

- Permission to hate.

- Permission to be yourself.

- Permission to hear the acceptance of another.

- Permission to have a self.

- Permission to fear and be afraid.

- Permission to withdraw.

- Permission to pretend.

- Permission to learn from yourself.

- Permission to comfort yourself.

- Permission to trust an adult.

- Permission to trust yourself.

- Permission to be.

- Permission to play.

PART 5

What the Future Will Bring

Whew! You have made it almost to the end of this workbook.

As we stated in the introduction, working with children isn't for everyone, doing play therapy isn't for everyone, and practicing child-centered play therapy isn't for everyone. The skills consistent with this approach will be valuable in your relationships, both personal and professional, with children and adults. You do not have to be a child-centered play therapist to be respectful and thoughtful in your relationships. We are certain that we are all capable of that. Many of you, however, will realize that child-centered play therapy makes sense for you and this is how you want to work clinically with children. Remember, to do this work in this way, you must embrace the philosophy. If you don't believe in the philosophy of child-centered play therapy, please do not try.

However, if you think you have found what you've been looking for, you'll still need to do these things:

1. Take a moment to review your own beliefs about children.

2. Write a letter. Not just any letter: After you have had a chance to practice child-centered play therapy for a while, we want you to write a letter to play therapy itself (Mullen, 2003a).

3. Get training and supervision. It's out there, and you don't have to look far. See Appendix C in this book, and check out the Association for Play Therapy's website at www.a4pt.org. We are committed to the preparation of play therapists, so if you cannot find training or supervision contacts, find us at the Integrative Counseling website: www.integrativecounseling.us.

What Do You Believe?

Remember that we said child-centered play therapy is a philosophy and not a set of techniques? Let's assess what you think, feel, and believe about children. Is your personal philosophy about children consistent with the child-centered approach? Have your beliefs changed as a result of your work throughout this book? In this section, we want you to take an honest look at your ability to follow through with child-centered play therapy as a therapeutic approach.

Your Turn: What Do You Believe?

Fill in the following blanks.

1. Children are _____.

2. Children like _____.

3. Children want _____.

4. Children believe _____.

5. Children wish _____.

6. Children have _____.

7. Children see _____.

8. Children try _____.

9. Children love _____.

10. Children hate _____.

11. Children need _____.

A Letter to Play Therapy

We have found it helpful to write a letter to play therapy as if it were a person, with human qualities. Our own letters, and letter from a budding play therapist, follow.

Dear Play Therapy:

Hi there again, old friend. I just wanted to write you a quick note to let you know how much I appreciate you. I certainly do not acknowledge enough how much you have impacted my life and the lives of others that I am connected with. I feel your impact personally and professionally each and every day.

Thank you for helping me to be a better parent and a better professional. I feel grounded in my work and in myself because you taught be about acceptance, patience, and understanding.

Sometimes I take you and all that you have taught me for granted. Lately, though, I have been reminded that you change lives and even save lives. It is my honor to be connected to you and share in the magic that surrounds you. Thank you for all you have done, all that you are doing, and all that you will do.

I love you,

Jodi

Dear Play Therapy:

Hey, BFF! I love getting together with you! We spend so much time together that people are starting to talk! All kidding aside, I am with you almost every day in one way or another. You make me feel proud and excited. Sometimes I think I know you so well, and then something will happen and I will learn something new and exciting about you. You are multifaceted and ever evolving—you keep me on my toes and never bore me. You have a way of helping me stay grounded and humble. I'm not sure how you do it, but you do. It's amazing how much power you have without ever having to exert your power. You are a constant reminder of the value of just being. So this is just a "shout out" to you for being in my life. I hope I can always do you the justice you deserve!

Love, your BFF,

June

Dear Play Therapy:

I am beyond happy I get to see you so often. Spending time with you helps me see children in a different light and appreciate them for all they have to offer. I can't believe how much I have changed and how much my relationships have changed since I met you. You have helped me connect and form relationships not only with children, but also adolescents and adults! You have taught me so many things and continue to help me learn and grow as a professional and person. You are something steady I can count on to help me influence change in children, and I am so thankful for that. You are positive, comforting, and accepting, and I hope all children get to experience you. Thank you for all your hard work, and I will see you soon!

Love,

Tiffany

Your Turn: A Letter to Play Therapy

Use the space provided to write your own letter to play therapy. After you have written your letter, read it to a supportive person in your life who will be excited about what you have learned for no other reason except that you are excited. If you do not have that person in your life at this moment, we would be honored for you to share your letter with us.

Dear Play Therapy:

Sample Answers

Here are our ideas of good therapeutic responses to the examples given. There are no specific "correct" answers. These responses are offered merely as examples.

Part 1: Why Empathy?

Your Turn: Translating Feelings Words

1. Annoyed

   "That *bothers* or *bugs* you."

   In dominant U.S. culture, a sigh or eye roll would convey that feeling.

2. Ashamed

   "You felt embarrassed."

3. Bored

   Yawn.

   "You are *tired* of this."

4. Brave

   "You feel like a *superhero*." If you say this, be careful not to give an example of a superhero. Most superheroes are male and Caucasian, and many children will not relate to the reference. Also, specific superheroes become outdated, and children may not recognize a particular superhero as such.

   "You're not scared."

5. Cooperative

   "You are *working* as part of a team."

   "You are *working* together with me."

6. Curious

   "You are *wondering*."

   "You're *unsure*."

7. Defective

   "You feel *broken,* like there's *something wrong* with you."

8. Disappointed

   "That's *upsetting.*"

   "Ugh."

   "You are feeling *sad* mixed with *mad.*"

9. Disconnected

   "It's like *no one cares.*"

   "You feel *lonely.*"

   "You feel *all alone.*"

10. Enthusiastic

    "Wow! You are *excited.*"

    "Yippee!"

11. Frustrated

    "Grrr!"

    "You are really *annoyed/fed up/mad.*"

12. Hopeless

    "You feel like *giving up.*"

    "You think, *why bother?*"

13. Insecure

    "You're *unsure* of yourself."

    "You don't feel like you *can.*"

14. Malicious

    "You feel *mean and sneaky.*"

    "You want others to *hurt.*"

15. Obstinate

In dominant U.S. culture, the gesture of folding arms over chest or stamping feet would work.

"You are *not going to move/stop/change.*"

"You're feeling *stubborn.*"

16. Overwhelmed

"This is *too much* for you."

Sigh.

In dominant U.S. culture, you could convey this feeling by putting your head down and shaking it "no."

17. Satisfied

"You're *all set/proud.*"

"Whoa."

18. Tentative

"You're *unsure.*"

"You want to *take your time.*"

19. Unpopular

"You feel like *no one likes you.*"

"You're feeling *left out.*"

20. Vulnerable

"It's all *scary.*"

"You're *not sure* you can *trust.*"

"You don't feel *safe.*"

Your Turn: Reflecting Feelings

1. You were very scared.   ☑ *You were afraid.*

2. You want that toy.   ☐ *You are determined.*

3. That was surprising.   ☑ *That was unexpected.*

4. You are so tired.   ☑ *You feel sloppy.*

5. You are sad.   ☑ *You are unhappy.*

6. That was a good one.   ☐ *You feel good about that.*

7. That shocked you.   ☑ *That was unbelievable.*

8. You feel like a superhero.   ☐ *You are feeling brave.*

9. You are angry.   ☑ *You are super mad.*

10. That was frustrating.   ☑ *You got fed up.*

Your Turn: Making Empathic Statements

1. Don't worry.   *Some things really worry you.*

2. It will be okay.   *You are scared things won't be okay.*

3. It's not a big deal.   *It's a big deal to you.*

4. You can't win them all.   *It's hard for you when you don't win.*

5. That's life.   *You feel that was unfair.*

6. It could be worse.   *It's really bad for you.*

7. You'll do fine.   *You're worried you won't do well.*

8. Everything will be all right.   *You're not sure things will work out.*

9. It's not that important.   *It's important to you.*

10. You'll get another chance.   *You are afraid you're not going to get another chance.*

11. Some problems solve themselves.   *This is a serious problem to you.*

13. There's always a bright side.   *You're not sure things will ever be better.*

14. People grow from experiences like this.   *This has been very hard for you.*

15. It's for your own good.   *You don't like what's happening.*

Part 2: The Child-Centered Approach

Your Turn: Is it Child Centered?

1. Client: (Looks around the playroom and finds an action figure he played with last session.)

   Therapist: You played with that last time, too.

   This is NOT child centered because the play therapist is referring to the last time the child played, which is not staying in the here and now. Child-centered play therapy takes place in the here and now. What happened in the past or what will happen in the future is not of concern to the play therapist.

   Alternative: You like that guy.

2. Client: (Picks up a feather boa, then looks frightened and throws it.) Ahhhhh!!! I don't like that!

   Therapist: You're really scared. Look, it's just a feather boa—it can't hurt you.

   This is NOT child centered. Although the play therapist is reflecting the child's feelings of being scared, the play therapist is also trying to make it better, thus minimizing the child's feelings.

   Alternative: You're really afraid of that!

3. Client: (Tries to shoot a basket several times and misses. Looks sad and stops trying.)

   Therapist: You almost got it that time—try again.

   This is NOT child centered because the play therapist is directing the session by telling the client to try again. The play therapist should be focusing attention to what the child is feeling in that moment. Also, what if the client doesn't want to try again? Then that expectation is put on the child.

   Alternative: You're bummed because you didn't get a basket.

4. Client: (On hearing that playtime is over) I didn't get a chance to play with that!

   Therapist: You can play with that next time if you want.

   This is NOT child centered because the play therapist is referring to next time, which is not staying in the here and now. It is also possibly putting an expectation on the child to play with the item next time.

   Alternative: You really wanted to play with that, but our playtime is over for today.

5. Client: (Gets to second level of a limit but does not reach the limit where she will be asked to leave the session.)

   Therapist: You're making good choices in here.

   This is NOT child centered because the play therapist is making a judgment by saying that the client is making good choices. It is not the play therapist's job to decide whether a child is making appropriate choices.

   Alternative: There is really no need to say anything to call attention to this. The child has decided to limit her own behavior.

6. Client: (Gets out the doctor kit and looks the pieces over, inspecting each one.)

   Therapist: It looks like you want to check me out.

   This is NOT child centered because the play therapist is making the assumption that the child wants to examine the play therapist with the doctor kit. If the child made a move toward the play therapist to examine the therapist, then this would be an appropriate response. We once supervised a play therapist who needed some nurturing herself. She would try to get those needs met in the playroom by creating situations like this.

   Alternative: Hmm. You're interested in that.

7. Client: Here's some for you and some for me. Let's eat.

   Therapist: You like to share with me.

   Bingo! Yes, this IS child centered!

8. Client: (Struggles with tape while making something.) This stupid tape isn't working.

   Therapist: Here—it looks like a stapler would do the job better.

   This is NOT child centered because in trying to make the job easier for the child, the play therapist is not allowing the child to experience the feelings that go along with not being able to do something. In order to know what frustration is, the child needs to experience it. If the play therapist jumps right in to solve the problem, this does not give the child the opportunity to work through those feelings. In this case, the play therapist is also depriving the child of the possible feeling of competence and pride after struggling and succeeding.

   Alternative: You are trying so hard to make that work.

9. Client: How do you spell *school?*

   Therapist: You want to know how to spell it: S-C-H-O-O-L.

This is NOT child centered because the play therapist is answering the child's question and not giving the child the opportunity to figure it out himself. In child-centered play therapy, the therapist does not correct the child or attempt to teach good spelling. In the playroom, the child can decide how to spell it.

Alternative: You're not sure how to spell it.

10. Client: I made this delicious soup for you. It has worms in it.

    Therapist: That's crazy. What kind of soup has worms in it?

    This is NOT child centered because the play therapist is not going with the child's lead. Instead, the play therapist is questioning what the child said and stifling the child's creativity.

    Alternative: Yuk! You really want to gross me out!

11. Client: I wish you were my mommy.

    Therapist: I can't be your mommy, but I can be your friend.

    This is NOT child centered because the play therapist is not cognizant of the child's feelings. This child obviously feels very connected to the play therapist. We have both had this said to us in session, and it is not an easy thing to hear!

    Alternative: You care about me so much that sometimes you wish I were your mommy.

12. Client: Hurry up and get me that basketball over there.

    Therapist: You like being able to tell me what to do.

    This IS child centered because the play therapist is reflecting the child's feelings. Many children love being in control in the playroom, and they love to use that control to the fullest. In general, children do not get many opportunities to be in control—play therapy gives them that opportunity. If a child feels that she has some semblance of control, she may not have to try as hard to gain it, a circumstance that usually translates into problem behavior.

13. Client: (Playing with figures in dollhouse) This boy is scared—he's hiding in the closet.

    Therapist: You're afraid.

    This is NOT child centered because the play therapist is making an interpretation that the child is identifying the figure as himself. The child has not said, "I am hiding in the closet." Instead, the child says "the boy." The play therapist needs to follow that lead, and until the client identifies the figure, it is just "the boy."

    Alternative: That boy is afraid. He doesn't want anyone to find him.

14. Client: (Using a male adult figure from the dollhouse) He's mad, so he's hitting the baby.

    Therapist: He's scary—just like your dad.

    Again, this is NOT child centered because the play therapist is making an interpretation. The client has not identified the figure as "dad"; therefore, it is just "him" or "that guy."

    Alternative: He's scary and really mean to that baby.

15. Client: (Looking closely at the dollhouse figures) Which one is supposed to be the mom?

    Therapist: Hmm . . . let's see. Which one looks like the mom to you?

    This is NOT child centered because the play therapist is not reflecting the child's feelings and is instead focused on trying to direct the child in figuring it out.

    Alternative: You're confused—you don't know which one is the mom.

16. Client: Aren't you supposed to be asking me questions?

    Therapist: You're confused—this is different from what you thought.

    This IS child centered. The play therapist is not attempting to answer the client's question and is instead reflecting the feelings behind the question. Many children are very surprised by the play therapy experience, especially if they have been to other counselors and have been asked a lot of questions. They are often relieved that play therapy is different. After Jodi said this to one client (a seven-year-old girl), she said, "Yes, this is very different." It was apparent that this was a relief to her, so the follow-up was "You like it that I'm not asking you questions." She replied, "You got that right!"

17. Client: Do you have any pink Play-Doh? I don't like this color.

    Therapist: I might—let me check. You don't like blue.

    This is NOT child centered because it is not the play therapist's job to please the client and get a color the child likes, nor is it child centered to name the color (blue). The client may think it's a different color. It is okay to name the color pink, as in the alternative, because the client has already identified the color as such.

    Alternative: You don't like that color and wish I had some pink Play-Doh.

18. Client: I don't know what to play with.

    Therapist: There are lots of things in here for you to do.

    This is NOT child centered because it is putting an expectation on the child to play, even though the child is unsure.

    Alternative: You just don't know where to start.

19. Client: I don't like these toys—they're stupid.

    Therapist: You don't like any of these things.

    This IS child centered because the play therapist is reflecting the client's dissatisfaction with the toys. The child could say this for many reasons, including testing to see what the play therapist will say or do if the child insults the therapist's toys. The reflection provided validates the child's feelings and does not attempt to direct the child to play. If the play therapist attempted to point out toys or direct the child to play with something, it would not be child centered; it would be more about the play therapist's need for the child to play than about the child's own issues.

20. Client: How much time is left? I'm not done.

    Therapist: You're concerned you won't be able to finish in time.

    This IS child centered because the play therapist is not answering the child's question as to how much time is left and is instead responding based on what may have prompted the child's question. Many children ask this question during their sessions. They begin to know how the session structure works and get worried that they will run out of time before they do all the work they need to do.

21. Client: Do other kids play in this room, too?

    Therapist: Yes, we have lots of kids that come here to play.

    This is NOT child centered because the play therapist is answering the child's question instead of reflecting what the child is feeling. Many children will ask this question because they want to think they're the only ones who have this special experience with you.

    Alternative: You're wondering if I only play with you.

22. Client: When am I going to see you next?

    Therapist: You will see me next week.

This is NOT child centered. Several things make this a weak response. The first is that the play therapist is answering the child's question instead of reflecting the child's feelings. The second is that it is best to refer to the next time you will see the child as "next time." You want to remain a person of your word, so what happens if something gets in the way of next week's session and you or the child can't make it?

Alternative: You want to know you'll be able to come back. I will see you next time.

23. Client: Can you open this for me?

Therapist: You think that's difficult and would like my help.

Yes, this IS child centered. The play therapist is reflecting that the child is having difficulty and has asked for help. In child-centered play therapy, the therapist follows the child's lead, so if the child asks for help, the play therapist does just that.

Part 3: Skills and Guidelines

Your Turn: Making Tracking Responses

1. Child stands on the chair.   *You are making yourself bigger.*

2. Child jumps up and down.   *You are showing me how you can jump.*

3. Child uses toy food to "feed" the baby doll.   *You're feeding that one.*

4. Child tries several crayons.   *You wanted to see if those work.*

5. Child looks out the window after hearing a sudden noise.   *You are going to see what that is all about.*

Your Turn: Responding to Questions

1. What time is it?   *You are concerned about the time.*

2. Do other kids come here?   *Sometimes you wonder if I play only with you.*

3. Do you have kids?   *You are curious about me.*

4. What's this toy called?   *You feel unsure.*

5. Why do you talk like that?   *It's annoying you.*

6. Can I swear in here?	*You aren't sure you can trust what I said about saying anything.*
7. Can I stay more minutes?	*You feel rushed, like you need more time.*
8. Why can't I spank you?	*You are confused why I won't let you hurt me.*
9. Do you love me?	*You are worried that I do not care about you.*
10. Can I leave now?	*You are feeling ready to go.*
11. Are you a boy or a girl?	*You are unsure about me.*
12. How come you're so fat?	*You're surprised.*
13. Would you like to see my penis?	*(Set the limit, then reflect this one.) Kyle, in this room you do not show your private parts. That would be unsafe. Your penis is private. You wanted to feel in charge.*
14. Your breath smells—what did you eat for lunch?	*You notice lots of things.*
15. Do you want to smell my fart?	*You want to know that I accept you no matter what.*

Your Turn: Responding to Directions

1. Child: Shut the lights, NOW!

   Therapist: (Turns off the lights.) You want to be in control.

2. Child: You close your eyes.

   Therapist: (Closes eyes.) You are uncomfortable that I see what you're doing.

3. Child: Please get me some more paper.

   Therapist: You are determined to finish what you were working on.

4. Child: Tell me I'm pretty.

   Therapist: You want me to say nice things about you.

5. Child: Pretend to eat this apple.

   Therapist: (Pretends to eat apple.)

6. Child: Give me that paintbrush.

   Therapist: You are sure you want me to get it for you, even though you can get it yourself.

7. Child: Tie my shoe.

   Therapist: You feel challenged and would like my help with that. It's difficult for you.

8. Child: Go sit in the corner.

   Therapist: (Goes and sits in the corner.) You want me to feel punished.

9. Child: Zip your mouth shut—no more talking!

   Therapist: I am really annoying you.

10. Child: Go over there and get me that truck.

    Therapist: You want to boss me around.

Your Turn: Should You Set the Limit?

Here we will try to explain why we would or would not set the limit. We will also offer an example of a limit with redirection. The redirection lets children know what they can do, and the limit emphasizes what they cannot do. There are many alternative redirections, and the goal here is to give you an idea. You will notice that for most examples, we have given you an example of how we would set the limit if indeed a limit needed to be set. You will also see that for many of the circumstances listed, there is no clear-cut answer.

1. Child wants to leave session early. (No)

   There is no reason to keep a child in the playroom if she wants to leave. It is important to recognize that keeping a child in the room will strain your relationship and is not therapeutic. Would you try to force an adult to stay in a therapy session if she wanted to leave? Probably not. Children rarely want to leave the playroom early, but when they do, it is important to honor their wish. This can be made less complicated by notifying caregivers and other stakeholders that children will sometimes need to leave early for therapeutic and safety reasons. Then if a child needs to leave or "limits out," someone will be waiting and will not be surprised if the child does not stay the full 30 minutes.

   > Limit: Rikki, you can leave now if you like, but that means we are not coming back into this special room today. (Make sure you let the child know that if she decides to leave, the session is over.)

2. Child wants to stand on the chair. (Yes/No)

This one is a judgment call. If you feel that the child can be safe, we do not see a reason to set the limit. We would make sure to stay close by in case the child gets wobbly and needs immediate physical support. You will find that children are attracted to standing on chairs and other structures. We think one reason is that they are not typically allowed to play in such a way; another is that kids like to make themselves bigger. The perspective from their culture is that power and control are connected to how big you are.

> Limit: Yuka, you cannot stand on the chair because it is unsafe, but you can raise your arms up high over your head if you want to be big.

3. Child spanks you. (Yes)

There is no reason to let a child hit or hurt you, but many children will attempt this behavior because that's the way they are or have been treated. Always limit this behavior.

> Limit: Danielle, you cannot hit or hurt me in here. You wanted me to feel what that's like. You can pretend to hit me or hit the doll instead.

4. Child tries to write on your (or his own) face with marker. (Yes/No)

We won't let children write on our faces with marker because we are just not comfortable having them do that. Never let a child do something to you in the playroom that makes you feel uncomfortable. When you feel uncomfortable, you are unable to adhere to the Eight Basic Principles. We will let children write on their own faces if they are not going back to class or somewhere other than home after their appointment. To go back to a public setting would be distracting and potentially embarrassing (even washable marker does not come off all the way).

> Limit: Alexandro, I see you want to decorate your face. You are feeling silly. One thing you cannot do in here is write on your face with markers. You can write on the paper or on the bop bag.

5. Child yells swear words. (Yes/No)

This depends on the setting. If you are in a setting where this would be an issue for confidentiality or a disturbance to others, then it would be appropriate to set the limit.

> Limit: Rory, you cannot yell those words in here. You can say them but not yell them. People walking by might get scared of those words.

6. Child wants to take clothes off. (Yes/No)

We will let children take off their shoes and socks. For some children, this is how they get or demonstrate that they are comfortable. We have had children in the playroom ask (and not ask) to take their clothes off. This makes the playroom a potentially unsafe place. We would never allow it.

> Limit: Jahleh, you are very hot in here today, but one thing you cannot do is take your shirt off. You can take your sneakers off if you want to.

7. Child plays with your hair. (Yes/No)

Jodi doesn't think you should allow this for hygiene reasons, but we include this example because it illustrates another reason to set limits: Having a child playing with your hair may actually be enjoyable, but the playroom is not a place to meet your own needs.

> Limit: Bailey, remember I told you there are some things you cannot do in here. One thing you cannot do is play with my hair. You wanted to show me you care about me. You can play with the doll's hair.

8. Child kisses you. (Yes)

As we have said before, the children you do play therapy with will love and adore you. We want to set good boundaries and not confuse them about the nature of our relationship, so we set the limit. It is, however, important to view this and the spectrum of behaviors displayed through a cultural lens. Please account for the culture of childhood and for individual children's salient cultural identifications.

> Limit: Paolo, remember I told you there are some things you cannot do in here. One thing you cannot do is kiss me on the face. I know you like me so much. You can blow me a kiss instead.

9. Child wants to tie you up. (Yes/No)

Here again, the decision has to do with your comfort level. We let kids tie us up because it does not bother either of us. Neither of us has ever felt as though we will not be able to react or get out. If you feel differently, then set the limit.

> Limit: Michael, remember there are some things you cannot do in here. You cannot tie me up. You can put the jump rope on me, and I will pretend I am tied up. You want me to feel trapped.

10. Child brings in toys from home. (No)

We do not limit this. We consider children bringing toys from home a gift. It is a way for children to share their bigger world with us. If the toy is dangerous, then we would set a limit.

> Limit: Noah, you are so proud of your new pocket knife, but that would make the playroom an unsafe place. You can have your dad hold it until our time is up.

11. Child wants to take home artwork. (Yes/No)

We will let children bring home paintings and drawings they have made, but not clay creations. (We would never have any clay if we allowed this!) We do not let children take home creations that have swear words or other hateful language written on them. Those words are allowed in the playroom only.

> Limit: Jess, you really want to take that picture home with you. That picture has to stay here because the words you wrote on it are only allowed in the special playroom. You can make a picture without those words and take it home.

12. Child sucks on a baby bottle. (No)

We see no reason to limit this behavior and, in fact, too often children are ridiculed for acting younger than they actually are. Remember, regression is a typical play style in the therapeutic playroom. Just make sure you keep the bottles sanitized.

> Limit: Andrea, you are really curious about that bottle. One thing you cannot do is put it in your mouth because I forgot to clean it. I will clean it now if you want so you can use it the way you want to.

13. Child shoots at you with toy gun. (Yes)

Even suction cup or foam darts can hurt. We do not let children shoot us or themselves in the playroom.

> Limit: Marty, remember I told you there some things you cannot do in here. One thing you cannot do is shoot me with the dart gun. I know you are so mad at me. You can shoot the walls or bop bag or dolls.

14. Child says nasty things to you. (No)

It is vitally important that children be able to say what they need to say in the playroom regardless of how rude it is. Remember, children often use harsh language because this language is what they are used to hearing. Children also want to make sure you understand their perspective, so many of them will treat you the way they feel they are treated.

Non-limit: Tiffany, you want me to know what it's like to be called names.

15. Child exposes her private parts. (Yes)

This may seem like a "no-brainer," but we want to make it very clear: There is no reason a child should be allowed to expose himself or herself in session. All of you will work with sexually abused children, whether you know it or not. Children who have been sexually abused are likely to have fragile boundaries. Some will show you their private parts because that is how other adults have engaged with them. Rather than deal with the anticipatory anxiety about their safety, they expose themselves to you as a subconscious test: "Can I trust this one (adult)?" When you set this limit, make sure you identify what private part you are talking about because many children who have been sexually victimized are not aware that parts of their bodies are private because their private parts have been made public. Even children who have not been sexually abused may expose themselves. The same limit should apply.

Limit: Alicia, there are some things you cannot do in here. You cannot pull down your pants and show me your vagina. Your vagina is a private part of your body. You were not sure if you could trust me not to hurt you. You can pull down the doll's pants.

Your Turn: No Questions

1.	Why did you do that?	*Sometimes you do things so fast you do not think about the consequences.*
2.	What could you have done differently?	*You came up with a solution.*
3.	How would you like to change this?	*This is not for you, and you wish there was another way.*
4.	Why do you think that happened?	*You are confused about why that happened.*
5.	Do you want me to color with you?	*I can't tell if you want me to color with you.*

Your Turn: No Praise

1. Greg: I did it. Do you like it?

   Praiser: I am so proud of you. It's awesome.

   Therapist: You are proud you did it and are curious what I think.

2. Jaielle: Here, catch.

   Praiser: That was a good throw.

   Therapist: You made it come right to me.

3. Eli: Look how tall I made the building.

   Praiser: Wow, you did a great job.

   Therapist: You are surprised about what you are able to do.

4. Juanita: (Puts on princess crown.) I am the fairest in the land.

   Praiser: You look beautiful.

   Therapist: You are feeling so pretty and special.

5. Griffin: (Draws a picture, looks at the therapist, and smiles.)

   Praiser: That's a terrific picture.

   Therapist: You are proud of what you created.

Part 4: Ready for Practice (and Play)

Your Turn: Name That Theme

1. Child repeatedly says to the play therapist, "Watch this!" or "Look!"

   Theme(s): This behavior could be seen as a child who is seeking attention and acceptance, but it could also be viewed as a child trying to gain control of the session.

   Response: "You want me to see all the cool things you can do."

2. Child uses items from the doctor kit and examines herself with the stethoscope.

   Theme(s): In this scenario, the child is showing self-nurturance by checking herself with the stethoscope.

   Response: "You are checking yourself out on the inside."

3. Child's dollhouse play consistently shows people or things falling off surfaces and in other precarious situations.

   Theme(s): Many children will act out situations like this in their dollhouse play, which often indicates the chaos, instability, and fear they are experiencing. This child could be showing the play therapist how overwhelmed he is in his life.

   Response: "That is a scary and dangerous place!"

4. Child punches and kicks the bop bag.

   Theme(s): Let's look at this scenario more closely: Suppose you are limited because you cannot see the child's face or demeanor. It is easy to immediately think that this child is angry and that this might possibly indicate a power and control and anger theme. But what if the child is smiling while punching or kicking the bop bag? What if the child is simply being goofy, punching the bop bag lightly to see it pop back up? What if the child is practicing karate moves on the bop bag? Would the theme still be anger or power and control? Probably not. The theme could be competency, or it could even be viewed as the child's way of connecting and building a relationship with you.

   Response: Your response would be based on what you are feeling and seeing in the session.

   Anger/power/control theme: "You want him to know you're the boss."

   Relationship/connecting theme: "You like to show me what you can do."

5. Child enters the playroom and wanders around calmly, checking out various items.

   Theme(s): Exploration is a very common theme that emerges right at the start of the play therapy process. The child in this scenario may simply be checking things out and getting a feel for the playroom.

   Response: "You are checking this room out."

6. Child alternates between attempting to do things for himself and asking for help.

   Theme(s): In this scenario, the child is demonstrating a balance between asking for help and attempting to do things for himself, which could indicate a dependence/independence theme. It could also indicate a theme of self-esteem/self-worth and suggest whether the child views himself as capable.

   Response: "Some things you can do by yourself, and other things you need my help with."

7. Child organizes the playroom.

   Theme(s): Sometimes children will organize the playroom because it helps to ease their anxiety. Other times, they may be trying to gain the play therapist's acceptance. Children may also want to gain control and are expressing this theme by putting items where they think they should go.

   Response: "You like things to be in the right place" or "You want to be helpful."

8. Child attempts to draw a picture but throws it away and starts again and again.

   Theme(s): By making attempt after attempt, this child could be indicating a theme of perfection. In this scenario, the child could be showing the play therapist how he feels about his ability to do things, which could indicate a theme of self-esteem.

   Response: "It bothers you when you can't do it the way you want."

9. Child repeatedly tells the play therapist what to do and how to do it.

   Theme(s): If you can't see the child's face or demeanor, there are many possibilities for themes. If the child appears angry and controlling, the theme could easily be power and control, anger, or betrayal. But what if the child's demeanor is pleasant and the instructions to the therapist are presented more as requests than as orders? It may still be the child's way of controlling the session but also be a way for the child to connect with you. This behavior could also indicate a theme of perfectionism—that the child needs things to be a certain way. Another theme could be anxiety, expressing the child's inability to play unless things are a certain way.

   Response: "You want me to know that you're the boss" or "You like me to do things a certain way."

10. Child attempts to undress the play therapist or self.

    Theme(s): Often this type of scenario indicates that a child is testing to see if she is safe in the playroom. This child may have precarious boundaries and is exposing herself or trying to undress the play therapist to see if the play therapist is a person she can trust.

    Response: First, limiting the behavior is necessary and then, "You wanted to see if you are safe in here."

Sample Answers   **123**

Your Turn: Commonly Asked Questions

1. What if the child will not talk?

   If a child chooses not to communicate verbally in child-centered play therapy, it is not a big deal. The play therapist is alert to respond to the child's facial expressions, body language, vocalizations, and play. Remember to watch the child's facial expressions and not only what he or she is playing with.

2. What if the child wants to bring in a friend, parent, sibling?

   We are reluctant to allow a child to bring a friend into the therapeutic playroom unless we have permission from the friend's parent. In clinical settings, we allow parents and siblings to join only the last five minutes, unless the intervention is intended to involve sibling play therapy or child-parent play therapy.

3. What about sand, paint, water, MESSES?

   The play therapist should not include any materials in playroom unless he or she can tolerate the potential mess they could make. Children need to make messes in play therapy to demonstrate chaos or as a metaphor for life's messes. Make sure to schedule ample time between sessions for cleaning up. Generally, playroom messes are taken care of by the play therapist. Kottman (2003) describes a collaborative clean-up as an alternative.

4. What do you do when the child won't leave the playroom?

   See page 58 for instructions on closing a session.

5. What about swearing, cussing, or hate language?

   In the playroom, children need to be able to say anything. Some children think "bad words" are words like *drunk, penis,* or *hate.* Typically, children do not use disturbing language, but there are some who are experts. These words have power, and children know that. When they use "bad language," it is helpful to view the situation through a lens of power. Do not use these words in your responses to children.

6. What about having toy guns in the playroom?

   Some settings, like schools, may not permit toy guns in the playroom. Some parents do not want their child to play with toy guns. Children will find a way to demonstrate aggression, even without toy guns, so they are not essential. However, it's good policy to alert parents that there are toy guns and other weapons in the playroom, should you choose to include them. Interestingly, we have had some children use the toy gun as a "nail gun" for construction play and as a fishing pole for competency play.

7. What if the child wants to leave the session early?

Very infrequently, a child will want to leave early. The child's wish should be honored and respected. In clinical settings, it's best to advise the person who has transported the child to session not to leave the premises so if the child limits out or chooses to leave the session early, that's possible. There is no reason to force a child to stay in session (you wouldn't insist that an adult stay, either). This may be a way the child can test the therapist or take control.

8. What about settings where noise in the playroom is a factor to others in close proximity?

Often, playrooms are located close to administrative offices or classrooms. Disturbing noise from the playroom can make adults and children outside it uncomfortable and subject the play therapist and children in treatment to unfavorable evaluation. In this case, it is helpful to limit not what children say, but how loudly they say it. We will let children pretend to yell or make loud noises but not at a level that would disturb others. This helps creates social awareness and empathy.

9. What if a child is being rude to the play therapist?

In the playroom, children often treat the play therapist in the ways they themselves are treated, and sometimes that means children will be rude and disrespectful. It is important to respond to the behavior and not the child. In many cases, children are testing: "If I am nasty to you, will you still care about me?"

10. What if the child tells others he or she can use bad words in session?

Children are usually amazed that they can say anything in the playroom. Some children will take you up on the offer to "say anything." Our experience generally is that most children do not take advantage of this privilege; however, they do recognize it is a privilege so they tend to brag about it and other aspects of play therapy to their peers.

11. What if a child puts toys in his or her mouth?

Take care in evaluating toys for choking hazard and do not include them in the room. It is important to keep toys clean and disinfected. Make determinations based on safety and hygiene.

12. What if a child breaks toys?

Toys will break, and children will have varying reactions in response, including fear, denial, even pleasure. It's important to reflect the feeling of the child. It is also important to be thoughtful about toys and not put expensive toys or toys you feel a sentimental attachment to in the playroom. Broken toys should be removed from the playroom because they can be dangerous; furthermore, broken toys send a message to children that the toys are not important.

13. What if a child wants to bring in a toy from home?

In our view, it is a gift when children bring a toy from home. The child is sharing part of home and revealing what is important. Even when children have brought hand-held video games, it has proven to be an opportunity to gain a deeper understanding of the child's phenomenological world.

14. What about interruptions from others during play therapy sessions?

When the play therapy session gets interrupted, we believe we owe the child that time. For example, if there is a fire drill and 12 minutes are taken up, we will say to the child, "Next time I need to give you some extra time because we got interrupted." If we are intruded on by an adult, for whatever reason, we will also give the child back the time: "Claire, I'm sorry the principal walked right into our session. I owe you time because that was your time to have my attention."

15. What if a child discloses abuse during a session?

Different settings have different policies about mandated reporting. Follow the protocol of your setting. In addition, realize that mandated reporters are not investigators. You do not need to determine whether the child has been abused, but you do need to assess for safety. It is important to remember your multiple roles here as mandated reporter and clinician. We stick to child-centered play therapy during the session and assess for imminent safety immediately following the session. We do not want to jeopardize the relationship with the child.

16. What if a child doesn't feel well and does not want to play or participate?

It's the child's choice whether to play or not. Follow the child's lead.

17. How can play therapists honor diversity?

Play therapists can honor diversity in many ways. Selection of toys can be a tangible and observable way of appreciating the richness of diversity. Multicultural dolls and dollhouse figures, food, kitchen tools, and musical toys are culturecentric. Play therapists should have an array of these toys. Gil and Drews (2005) provide additional suggestions in their book *Cultural Issues in Play Therapy.*

18. What do you do when a child tells you he or she loves you?

As a play therapist, you will be a very special person to children. You can expect that children will love you and tell you so. Although you may care for, even love, your child clients, it would at best be confusing for you to disclose such feelings to them. Here again, it is best to stick to the process of child-centered play therapy: Respond to the child through a listening response such as "You really care for me" or "You feel so connected to me."

19. What should you do if the child falls asleep in session?

To fall asleep, a child must feel very safe and, of course, very tired. It would not be therapeutic to awaken him. He is getting a basic need met. Let him sleep until the five-minute warning.

Your Turn: Evaluating Therapist Responses

Behavior	Accurate	Inaccurate	Therapeutic	Non-therapeutic	Tolerable	Threatening
1. Child moves closer to play therapist.	☑	☐	☑	☐	☑	☐

When the play therapist makes a response that the child views as representing her thoughts or feelings, the child may respond by moving closer in proximity to the play therapist.

2. Child moves away from play therapist.	☑	☑	☐	☑	☐	☑

Conversely, if the child experiences the response of the play therapist as inaccurate, nontherapeutic, or threatening, the child is likely to increase the physical distance between himself and play therapist. It's the child's way of saying, "That response didn't work." If the response was accurate, the play therapist may have made the response before the child could handle it.

3. Play intensifies.	☑	☑	☑	☑	☑	☐

Play may intensify because the therapist has made either a therapeutic or nontherapeutic response. On the one hand, the child's play may intensify when the therapist's response is accurate because the child feels validated and is excited to recognize that her communication was successful. The child experiences what the play therapist says as safe and therefore intensifies the play to show the therapist the degree of what she is feeling. On the other hand, the child's play may intensify when the play therapist is inaccurate as a mean of reiterating the communication. It's the child's way of saying it again, and louder, hoping that the therapist will "get it" this time. It is the play therapist's responsibility to read the contextual cues to determine the reason the play intensified and to apply child-centered play therapy principles accordingly.

Behavior	Accurate	Inaccurate	Therapeutic	Non-therapeutic	Tolerable	Threatening
4. Child uses play therapist's words.	☑	☐	☑	☐	☑	☐

Children will use the words of the play therapist when they feel connected to the play therapist. This happens as a result of the therapist's reflecting the child's feelings accurately and making responses that help the child heal, grow, or change. It also indicates that the therapist's actions are tolerable to the child and do not push the child to adhere to an adultcentric agenda or pace.

Behavior	Accurate	Inaccurate	Therapeutic	Non-therapeutic	Tolerable	Threatening
5. Child corrects play therapist.	☐	☑	☑	☐	☐	☑

If a child corrects the play therapist, it is likely that the play therapist's response was inaccurate. Feeling safe and sure enough to correct an adult is likely to happen in a therapeutic moment. A child also may correct the play therapist because the play therapist has stripped the child's protective defenses and, therefore, the child views the play therapist's response as threatening. The child corrects the play therapist as a way of recreating the defense.

Behavior	Accurate	Inaccurate	Therapeutic	Non-therapeutic	Tolerable	Threatening
6. Child turns away from play therapist.	☑	☑	☐	☑	☐	☑

Sometimes the play therapist will move too quickly or deeply in his or her reflections of feeling. This can be unsettling for children. The child may meet both inaccurate and accurate responses by turning away from the therapist. Turning away is more typical of inaccurate or threatening responses but is also indicative of accurate responses that are "too deep, too soon."

Behavior	Accurate	Inaccurate	Therapeutic	Non-therapeutic	Tolerable	Threatening
7. Child invites play therapist into play.	☑	☐	☑	☐	☑	☐

Children will include the play therapist in their play if they feel safe, comfortable, listened to, and understood.

Behavior	Accurate	Inaccurate	Therapeutic	Non-therapeutic	Tolerable	Threatening
8. Child tells play therapist to shut up, stop talking.	☑	☑	☐	☑	☐	☑

This kind of reaction to the play therapist's responses usually means that the therapist's response is off target, nontherapeutic, and scary to the child. It may also be the reaction of the child who cannot tolerate having his feelings reflected back to her. Jodi had this happen regularly with a child she worked with who was bent on not feeling. When Jodi continued to reflect her feelings, even saying, "You hate feeling," she taped Jodi's mouth shut.

Behavior	Accurate	Inaccurate	Therapeutic	Non-therapeutic	Tolerable	Threatening
9. Child nods "yes" after response.	☑	☐	☑	☑	☑	☐

This is another behavior where subculture and context play a huge role in the accurate assessment of the interplay between the play therapist's response and the child's response. The child may agree because he feels validated or because he thinks he should not acknowledge that you are wrong or because what you just said felt therapeutic or because what you said seemed insensitive but the child believes he is supposed to agree with his elders. This child could say yes because that's how he responds when an adult says anything to him and he is scared to say no or because you have not demonstrated to him that you accept him as he is. As you can see, these behaviors and what they may mean in the playroom are embedded in context.

Behavior	Accurate	Inaccurate	Therapeutic	Non-therapeutic	Tolerable	Threatening
10. Child wants to end session.	☑	☑	☐	☑	☐	☑

This can be a behavioral response to an accurate response on the part of the play therapist, or it can be a way for the child to communicate that the play therapist went too deep, too soon. It also may be the child's way of demonstrating that she does not feel understood, respected, accepted or even safe.

Behavior	Accurate	Inaccurate	Therapeutic	Non-therapeutic	Tolerable	Threatening
11. Child's play changes abruptly.	☑	☑	☑	☑	☑	☑

The child's play is typically additive if you are accurate, therapeutic, and/or making tolerable responses. Just because the child's play changes abruptly does not mean the opposite assessment should be made. Children's play can change abruptly for any of the following reasons, among others: the child becomes distracted by another toy, feels pressured to play with a particular toy, feels validated, feels misunderstood, feels safe to try something new, or feels threatened and tries to achieve a sense of safety and security by changing play.

Behavior	Accurate	Inaccurate	Therapeutic	Non-therapeutic	Tolerable	Threatening
12. Child's play is additive.	☑	☐	☑	☐	☑	☐

Children's play is communication; therefore, adding to their play is adding to their story. Children won't "tell" you more if you are not making accurate, therapeutic, and tolerable responses.

Behavior	Accurate	Inaccurate	Therapeutic	Non-therapeutic	Tolerable	Threatening
13. Child smiles.	☑	☑	☑	☑	☑	☑

Subculture and context play a huge role in the accurate assessment of the interplay between the play therapist's response and the child's response. The child may smile because he feels validated, because he thinks it's funny that you are wrong, because what you just said felt therapeutic, or because what you said seemed stupid and had no therapeutic value. The child could smile because that's how he responds when an adult says anything to him or because you demonstrated to him that you accept him as he is. These behaviors and what they may mean in the playroom are embedded in context.

Behavior	Accurate	Inaccurate	Therapeutic	Non-therapeutic	Tolerable	Threatening
14. Child looks at the play therapist.	☑	☑	☑	☐	☑	☐

Children typically will make eye contact with the play therapist when they feel safe, accepted, and heard. Some children may also use prolonged eye contact to suggest to the play therapist that the therapist's response is inaccurate and they feel angry, although in our experience it is rare that eye contact is a sign of inaccuracy versus accuracy.

Behavior	Accurate	Inaccurate	Therapeutic	Non-therapeutic	Tolerable	Threatening
15. Child ignores the play therapist.	☑	☑	☐	☑	☐	☑

Sometimes the child will ignore you because (this should sound familiar) you made a response that scares the child because it went too deep, too soon. However, for the most part this kind of behavioral reaction by a child to the play therapist would suggest that the play therapist did not communicate empathic understanding, unconditional positive regard, or acceptance. The child is left feeling disconnected, unheard, and unsafe.

Forms and Checklists

In this appendix, we have gathered some helpful forms and checklists. We discovered that typical clinical case notes were not serving us well, so we developed our own Child-Centered Play Therapy Session Clinical Notes form, reproduced here. Our goal in developing and implementing this form was to make it easy to assess for growth as well as to aid in consultation with other professionals.

It is common to be the only play therapist in an agency or school. Although there may be other mental health professionals working in the same setting as you, the foundation of specialized training in play therapy may be yours alone. In addition to receiving regular supervision from credentialed play therapist supervisors who are trained in both play therapy and supervision, we use the Self-Supervision Form for Child-Centered Play Therapy Sessions to help us assess our own sessions. We trust you will find the form a useful tool.

The final item is a brief version of the Child-Centered Play Therapy Implementation Checklist, originally devised by Mullen and Uninsky (2007). After you complete this workbook, it may be helpful to use the checklist as a tool to gauge your adherence to the child-centered play therapy model. It would be appropriate to share this information in peer or clinical supervision contexts as you begin to integrate what you have learned.

Child-Centered Play Therapy Session Clinical Notes

Client name _____ Date _____ Time of session _____

Counselor _____ Session no. _____ Length of session _____

Transitioned into session

☐ enthusiastically ☐ wearily ☐ anxiously ☐ irritably ☐ tentatively ☐ excitedly

☐ boastfully ☐ begrudgingly ☐ calmly ☐ inquisitively ☐ merrily ☐ _____

as evidenced by _____

Toys used

☐ action heroes/soldiers

☐ cars/trucks

☐ animals: domestic, zoo, dinosaurs, _____

☐ bop bag/egg cartons/socker bopper

☐ dress-ups/masks

☐ water

☐ baby dolls/bottle

☐ telephone

☐ camera

☐ dollhouse/small figures

☐ guns/handcuffs/rope

☐ puppets

☐ crayons/markers/whiteboard/paint

☐ swords/noodles/shields

☐ kitchen/dishes/food

☐ sand/miniatures

☐ doctor kit

☐ money/cash register

☐ blocks/Legos

☐ basketball/hoop/balls

☐ _____

Themes

☐ helpless/inadequacy

☐ loneliness

☐ aggression/revenge

☐ confusion

☐ self-esteem/self-worth

☐ fears/anxiety

☐ safety/security/protection

☐ good versus evil

☐ nurturing/self-care/healing

☐ anger/sadness

☐ death/loss/grieving

☐ trust/betrayal

☐ _____

☐ _____

Subjective feelings expressed

HAPPY: relieved, satisfied, pleased, delighted, excited, surprised, silly, _____

SAD: disappointed, hopeless, pessimistic, discouraged, lonely, _____

ANGRY: impatient, annoyed, frustrated, mad, mean, jealous, _____

AFRAID: vulnerable, helpless, distrustful, _____

Session narrative

Include subjective feelings and themes, significant verbalizations, "firsts," additive or cycling play, description of role, or other content.

_____

_____

_____

_____

_____

Prosocial behaviors displayed

☐ manners   ☐ care taking   ☐ self-control

☐ sharing   ☐ respect   ☐ picking up

☐ empathy   ☐ mutuality   ☐ apologizing

☐ problem solving   ☐ _____   ☐ _____

Limits set and response of the child

_____

_____

_____

Transitioned out of session

☐ enthusiastically   ☐ wearily   ☐ anxiously   ☐ irritably   ☐ tentatively   ☐ excitedly

☐ boastfully   ☐ begrudgingly   ☐ calmly   ☐ inquisitively   ☐ merrily   ☐ _____

as evidenced by _____

Reminders/other notes

_____

_____

_____

_____

Self-Supervision Form for Child-Centered Play Therapy Sessions

Date _____ Date of review _____

Child's name _____ Age _____ Session no. _____

1. List feelings expressed by the child. Put an "X" next to feelings you reflected. Put an "O" next to feelings you could have reflected.

☐	_____	☐	_____
☐	_____	☐	_____
☐	_____	☐	_____
☐	_____	☐	_____
☐	_____	☐	_____
☐	_____	☐	_____
☐	_____	☐	_____
☐	_____	☐	_____
☐	_____	☐	_____
☐	_____	☐	_____

2. My overall responses to child's feelings. Give examples and evidence.

    - Were they accurate?
    - Were they complete?
    - Were they timed appropriately?

    _____

    _____

3. Which of the child's feelings, if any, did I not respond to appropriately?

    _____

    _____

From *Child-Centered Play Therapy Workbook,* © 2014 by J.A. Mullen and J.M. Rickli, Champaign, IL: Research Press (www.researchpress.com, 800-519-2707).

4. What kind of error was committed in responding inappropriately? (Give specific examples.)

- Failure to respond at all.
- Failure to respond until much later.
- Addressing action instead of feeling.
- Mislabeling of feelings.
- Failure to match own degree of emotion with that expressed by child.

_____

_____

5. Frequency of responses. (Give specific examples.)

- Balanced.
- Too few responses made to demonstrate understanding and acceptance of child.
- Too much talking.
- Failure to make succinct responses.
- Play-by-play description.
- Too much interest to unimportant details.
- Other?

_____

_____

6. Were limits enforced appropriately?

- Too many. (What's the evidence?)
- Too few. (How do you know?)
- Not enforced? (Why not?)
- Other?

_____

_____

7. Was structuring provided appropriately? (How do you know?)

- Opening
- Five minutes
- One minute
- Closing
- Was timing appropriate?

_____

_____

8. Was factual information provided appropriately? If not, how was the error made?

- Refused to provide an answers, reflecting child's wish for an answer beyond a reasonable point.
- Too much information provided, more than required.
- Misleading information provided, avoiding facing the truth.

_____

_____

9. Proximity

- Too close.
- Too far away.
- Child looked uncomfortable with distance.
- Adult looked uncomfortable with distance.

_____

_____

10. Language

Adult used language appropriate for the child's age and cognitive development.

Give three examples.

_____

_____

11. Control of adult's feelings. Give examples.

- Adequate.
- Own opinions, evaluations, judgments crept in.
- Voice revealed contradictory feelings.
- Appeared uninterested, distracted.

_____

_____

12. Adult carried off technique(s) comfortably? If not, what was evidence to suggest otherwise?

- Adult seemed uncomfortable. How?
- Child criticized or rebuffed technique(s).

_____

_____

13. Adult is comfortable with child's direction of the session. Does not attempt to divert by open or subtle means. If not, explain the error.

_____

_____

14. Apparent themes in the child's play.

_____

_____

15. What did you like about the child?

_____

_____

16. What about this child reminds you of yourself?

_____

_____

17. What's your overall feeling about the session?

_____

_____

18. Most positive aspect of session.

_____

_____

19. Aspects to work on.

_____

_____

20. How was the process of completing this supervision form for you?

_____

_____

Additional notes

Child-Centered Play Therapy Implementation Checklist

Level of Strategy Implementation

Program Area/Quality Indicator	None	Minimal	Moderate	Complete	Exemplary
1. Introduction to Therapy					
Implementation Indicator 1.1: Building rapport with the client	①	②	③	④	⑤
The therapist establishes a trusting relationship with the participating child.					
Implementation Indicator 1.2: Assuring confidentiality	①	②	③	④	⑤
The therapist successfully assures the parent(s) or caregiver(s) that all information disclosed will be kept strictly confidential. The therapist also assures the participating client, but only if he or she is capable of understanding the issues relating to confidentiality.					
Implementation Indicator 1.3: Gathering background information	①	②	③	④	⑤
The therapist collects information in a comprehensive manner to permit a thorough understanding of the phenomenological perspective of the child.					
Implementation Indicator 1.4: Orientation to the program	①	②	③	④	⑤
The therapist provides an introduction to child-centered play therapy, highlighting the key features and articulating the expected course of the intervention.					
Implementation Indicator 1.5: Encouraging involvement	①	②	③	④	⑤
The therapist uses a variety of techniques (including the use of toys) to facilitate child involvement, play, and verbalizations.					

From *Child-Centered Play Therapy Workbook*, © 2014 by J. A. Mullen and J. M. Rickli, Champaign, IL: Research Press (www.researchpress.com, 800-519-2707).

Program Area/Quality Indicator	Level of Strategy Implementation				
	None	Minimal	Moderate	Complete	Exemplary
Implementation Indicator 1.6: Developing and using an appropriate play therapy environment	①	②	③	④	⑤
The therapist introduces and uses appropriate playroom materials.					

2. Treatment

	None	Minimal	Moderate	Complete	Exemplary
Implementation Indicator 2.1: Structuring the relationship	①	②	③	④	⑤
The therapist introduces the parameters and nature of the play therapy relationship.					
Implementation Indicator 2.2: Acknowledging the culture of children	①	②	③	④	⑤
The therapist acknowledges and demonstrates appreciation of the developmental and sociocultural perspectives of the child.					
Implementation Indicator 2.3: Role-playing to identify feelings, and behaviors	①	②	③	④	⑤
The therapist and the child engage in role-play to help the child identify feelings and behaviors.					
Implementation Indicator 2.4: Establishing limits	①	②	③	④	⑤
The therapist sets limits, as needed, to provide additional structure to sessions and to maintain safety.					
Implementation Indicator 2.5: Therapeutic responses	①	②	③	④	⑤
The therapist provides ongoing responses calibrated to help the child in feeling understood, in becoming aware of his or her responsibility in the therapeutic relationship, and in gaining insight into his or her behavior.					

Level of Strategy Implementation

Program Area/Quality Indicator	None	Minimal	Moderate	Complete	Exemplary
Implementation Indicator 2.6: Role-playing and play to improve coping skills The therapist and the child act out scenarios to provide an opportunity for the child to practice coping skills and to utilize a problem-solving approach to difficult situations.	①	②	③	④	⑤
Implementation Indicator 2.7: Outcome indicators for clients with family problems When family problems are diagnosed, the therapist works to establish a range of outcomes intended to improve, where needed, the child's communication, relational, and coping skills.	①	②	③	④	⑤
Implementation Indicator 2.8: Outcome indicators for clients with educational problems When educational problems are indicated, the therapist works to establish a range of outcomes intended to improve, where needed, the child's communication, relational, and coping skills.	①	②	③	④	⑤
Implementation Indicator 2.9: Outcome indicators for clients with mental health problems When mental health problems are diagnosed, the therapist works to establish a range of outcomes intended to improve, where needed, the child's communication, social, and emotional coping skills.	①	②	③	④	⑤

Pathways to Advanced Training and Credentialing

You are off to a great start!

You have taken a big step to become a stronger clinician, more skilled in helping children and providing quality play therapy. The ripple effect in terms of your professional development, children, and families means communities will be impacted by your commitment to professional growth and excellence. That's a big deal!

The next step for professionals who are ready to unlock the highest degree of play therapy skills and practice is to become a credentialed play therapist. There are two different credentials in play therapy available to those who seek to enhance their play therapy work. Although they both designate advanced training in play therapy, they are very different in terms of depth and concentration.

The Certified Child-Centered Play Therapist (CCPT) credential is earned through an organization called the National Institute of Relationship Enhancement (NIRE). As discussed earlier in this workbook, this credential allows you to be fully grounded in one particular theory: child-centered play therapy. The benefits of being grounded in a particular theory are discussed in the introduction of this workbook. This route requires you to already have or be enrolled in a master's degree program. It involves submitting 26 videorecorded play therapy sessions to an approved supervisor. The supervisor views the sessions and then provides individual or group supervision for each session. It is an intensive study in child-centered play therapy. The details follow:

National Institute of Relationship Enhancement (NIRE) Certification in Child-Centered Play Therapy

- This program leads to certification in child-centered play therapy.

- Credential earned: CCPT (Certified Child-Centered Play Therapist)

- Credential of Supervisor: CCPT-S (Certified Child-Centered Play Therapist Supervisor)

Program requirements: In order to enroll in the program, individuals must submit an application, have an earned master's degree in a helping profession OR be currently enrolled in such a program, and have had a three-credit graduate level course in play therapy or the equivalent in workshops.

Parameters of the program: Supervisees submit recorded sessions for review by a supervisor. Supervisees earn a minimum of 26 hours of clinical supervision. Supervision can be face to face, through video calls, and/or via phone. Individual and group supervision formats are allowed.

Fees: There is an application fee (for the most accurate fee, see www.nire.org) and fees for supervision that are set by NIRE, but supervisors are able to set fees independently.

Once you earn the CCPT, you are now well on your way to satisfying the requirements for an RPT credential. The credential Registered Play Therapist (RPT) is earned through the Association for Play Therapy. This credential requires professionals to have completed a master's degree and be licensed in their state in order to apply. It weighs more heavily on continuing education hours than on individual supervision. It is a well-respected credential, although it does not focus on any one particular theory. The requirements and process are highlighted as follows.

Association for Play Therapy (APT) Certification in Play Therapy

- This program leads to certification in play therapy.

- Credential earned: RPT (Registered Play Therapist)

- Credential of supervisor: RPT-S (Registered Play Therapist Supervisor)

Program requirements: To enroll in the program individuals must submit an application, have an earned master's degree in a helping profession, hold a license or certification in said helping profession, and have coursework in play therapy or the equivalent in workshops (150 continuing education hours). See the APT website for further explanation and clarification (www.a4pt.org).

Parameters of the program: Supervisees will earn a minimum number of continuing education hours in play therapy. Clinical supervision is also necessary and can be face to face, through video calls, and/or via phone. Individual and group supervision formats are allowed.

Fees: There is an application fee (for the most accurate fee, see www.a4pt.org). Fees for supervision are set by supervisors.

References and Bibliography

Albon, S. L. (1996). The therapeutic action of play. *Journal of the American Academy of Child and Adolescent Psychiatry, 35*(4), 545–548.

Axline, V. M. (1947). *Play therapy.* New York: Ballantine.

Axline, V. M. (1969). *Play therapy* (Rev. ed.). New York: Ballantine

Clark, A. J. (2010). Empathy and sympathy: Therapeutic distinctions in counseling. *Journal of Mental Health Counseling, 32,* 95.

Cochran, N. H., Nordling, W. J., & Cochran, J. L. (2010). *Child centered play therapy.* Hoboken, NJ: Wiley.

Erdman, P., & Lampe, R. (1996). Adapting basic skills to counsel children. *Journal of Counseling and Development, 74,* 374–377.

Fiorini, J., & Mullen, J. (2006). *Counseling children and adolescents through grief and loss.* Champaign, IL: Research Press

Gil, E., & Drewes, A. A. (2005). *Cultural issues in play therapy.* New York: Guilford.

Ginott, H. G. (1961). *Group psychotherapy with children.* New York: McGraw–Hill.

Killough-McGuire, D., & McGuire, D. E. (2001). *Linking parents to play therapy: A practical guide with applications, interventions, and case studies.* Philadelphia: Brunner-Routledge.

Kottman, T. (1999). Play therapy. In A. Vernon (Ed.), *Counseling children and adolescents* (2nd ed.). Denver, CO: Love Publishing.

Kottman, T. (2003). *Partners in play: An Adlerian approach to play therapy* (2nd ed.). Alexandria, VA: American Counseling Association.

Kottman, T. (2010). *Play therapy: Basic and beyond.* Alexandria, VA: American Counseling Association.

Kranz, P. L, & Lund, N. L. (1993). Axline's eight principles of play therapy revisited. *International Journal of Play Therapy, 2*(2), 53–60.

Lambert, M. J., & Cattani-Thompson, K. (1996). Current findings regarding the effectiveness of counseling: Implications for practice. *Journal of Counseling and Development, 74,* 601–608.

Landreth, G. L. (2002). *Play therapy: The art of the relationship* (2nd ed.). New York: Brunner-Routledge.

Landreth, G. L., & Wright, C. S. (1997). Limit setting practices of play therapists in training and experienced play therapists. *International Journal of Play Therapy, 6,* 41–62.

Mann, D. (1996). Serious play. *Teacher's College Record, 97*(3), 446-449.

McCalla, C. L. (1994). A comparison of three play therapy theories: Psychoanalytical, Jungian, and client-centered. *International Journal of Play Therapy, 3*(1), 1–10.

Moustakas, C. E. (1953). *Children in play therapy: A key to understanding normal and disturbed emotions.* New York: McGraw-Hill.

Mullen, J. A. (2003a). Dear Play Therapy. *Association for Play Therapy Newsletter, 22*(4), 11–12.

Mullen, J. A. (2003b). Speaking of children: A study of how play therapists make meaning of children. *Dissertation Abstracts International, 64,* 11A.

Mullen, J. A., & Grimshaw-Clark, M. C. (2002). Parent and play therapist: Addressing duality. *Association for Play Therapy Newsletter, 21*(4), 25–26.

Mullen, J. A., & Rickli, J. (2011). *How play therapists can engage parents and professionals.* Oswego, NY: Integrative Counseling Services.

Mullen, J. A., & Uninsky, P. (2007). *Child-Centered Play Therapy Fidelity Checklist.* Hamilton, NY: Youth Policy Institute.

Nordling, W. J., & Guerney, L. (1999). Typical stages in the child-centered play therapy process. *The Journal for the Professional Counselor, 14*(1), 17–23.

Oaklander, V. (1988). *Windows to our children.* (4th ed.). Highland, NY: The Gestalt Journal Press.

O'Connor, K. J. (2000). *The play therapy primer* (2nd ed.). Wiley.

Orton, G. L. (1996). *Strategies for counseling with children and their parents.* Pacific Grove, CA: Brooks/Cole.

Pedersen, P. B., & Ivey. A. (1993). *Culture-centered counseling and interviewing skills.* Westport, CT: Praeger.

Phillips, E., & Mullen, J. A. (1999). Client-centered play therapy techniques for elementary school counselors: Building the supportive relationship. *The Journal for the Professional Counselor, 14,* 25–36.

Ray, D. (2004). Supervision of basic advanced skills in play therapy. *Journal of Professional Counseling: Practice, Theory, and Research, 32*(2), 28–41.

Ray, D. (2011). *Advanced play therapy: Essential conditions, knowledge, and skills for child practice.* Milton Park, Oxfordshire, England: Taylor and Francis.

Rogers, C. R. (1951). *Client-centered therapy: Its current practice, implications and theory.* Boston: Houghton Mifflin.

Roopnarine, J. L., Johnson, J. E., & Hooper, F. H. (Eds.). (1994). *Children's play in diverse cultures.* Albany: State University of New York Press.

Stern, M., & Newland, L. M. (1994). Working with children: Providing a framework for the roles of counseling psychologists. *The Counseling Psychologist, 22*(3), 402–425.

Tanner, Z., & Mathis, R. D. (1995). A Child-centered typology for training novice play therapists. *International Journal of Play Therapy, 4*(2), 1–13.

Thompson, C. L., & Rudolph, L. B. (2000). *Counseling children* (5th ed.). Stamford, CT: Brooks/ Cole.

VanFleet, R., Sywulak, A. E., & Caparosa, C. (2010). *Child-centered play therapy.* New York: Guilford.

Vargas, L. A., & Koss-Choino, J. D. (1992). *Working with culture: Psychotherapeutic interventions with ethnic minority children and adolescents.* San Francisco: Jossey-Bass.

About the Authors

Jodi Ann Mullen, PhD, LMHC, NCC, RPT-S, CPT-S, is the director of Integrative Counseling Services, PLLC, in Auburn, Cicero, and Oswego, New York. She is an associate professor at SUNY Oswego in the Counseling and Psychological Services Department, where she is the coordinator of the Mental Health Counseling Program and Graduate Certificate Program in Play Therapy. Dr. Mullen is a credentialed play therapist and play therapy supervisor. She is the author of several manuscripts on play therapy, child counseling, and supervision. Her books include *Counseling Children and Adolescents Through Grief and Loss* (with Dr. Jody Fiorini, 2006), *Supervision Can Be Playful: Techniques for Child and Play Therapist Supervisors* (co-edited with Athena Drewes, 2008), *Counseling Children: A Core Issues Approach* (2011), and *How Play Therapists Can Engage Parents and Professionals* (with June Rickli, 2011). With her family, she recently authored *Naughty No More: A Workbook to Help Kids Make Good Decisions* (2013). Dr. Mullen is on the editorial board for the *International Journal of Play Therapy* and is a past clinical editor of *Play Therapy Magazine.* She was the 2008 recipient of the Key Award for Professional Training and Education through the Association for Play Therapy. She is also an international speaker, avid runner, and proud mother of Andrew and Leah.

June M. Rickli, RRP, CCPT, CCPT-S, is assistant director at Integrative Counseling Services, PLLC, in Oswego, New York. She received her bachelor's degree in psychology and master's degree in mental health counseling from SUNY Oswego. She is credentialed as a registered play therapist through the Association for Play Therapy and as a child-centered play therapist and child-centered play therapist supervisor through the National Institute of Relationship Enhancement. She has presented workshops on play therapy throughout New York State. In addition to presenting, she also teaches at the graduate level in the Counseling and Psychological Services Department at SUNY Oswego. At Integrative Counseling Services, she provides play therapy services to children and counseling services to adults and adolescents, and is responsible for the supervision and management of graduate interns. She co-wrote *How Play Therapists Can Engage Parents and Professionals* (2011) with Dr. Jodi Mullen, has three grown children (two sons and a daughter), and is a proud grandmother to three granddaughters.